VENICE

VENICE

The Art of Living

Text by Frédéric Vitoux

Photography by Jérôme Darblay

in collaboration with Nanou Billault

Translated by Alexandra Bonfante-Warren

STEWART, TABORI & CHANG

NEW YORK

Copyright © 1990 Flammarion

Published in 1991 by
Stewart, Tabori & Chang, Inc.
575 Broadway, New York, New York 10012

Vitoux, Frédéric.
    [Venise, l'art de vivre. English]
    Venice, the art of living / Frédéric Vitoux; photographs by
Jérôme Darblay; with the collaboration of Nanou Billault.
        p.   cm.
    Translation of: Venise, l'art de vivre.
    Includes index.
    ISBN 1-55670-206-X
    1. Venice (Italy)—Social life and customs. 2. Venice (Italy)—
Social life and customs—Pictorial works. I. Darblay, Jérôme.
II. Billault, Nanou.   III. Title.
DG675.6.V5813   1991
945'.31—dc20   90-49053
                    CIP

Distributed in the U.S. by Workman Publishing,
708 Broadway, New York, New York 10003
Distributed in Canada by Canadian Manda Group,
P.O. Box 920 Station U, Toronto, Ontario M8Z 5P9.
Distributed in the U.K. territories by Little,
Brown and Company, International Division,
34 Beacon Street, Boston, Massachusetts 02108

Printed in Italy

0 9 8 7 6 5 4 3 2 1

Map on page 246–47 by Léonie Schlosser

Design by Marc Walter

CONTENTS

PREFACE

Venice is an extraordinary city. Everyone knows of it, everyone imagines it. It is difficult to see Venice with a fresh eye, unencumbered by reputation and much-handled images. No other city is so well known and still so secret. Venice reveals itself only to the patient and perceptive visitor, jealously guarding its mystery, its soul. Despite the hundreds of thousands of tourists who walk its streets each year, the city shields its inner truth. A phrase of Simone Weil's comes to mind: "a human medium of which one is as unaware as of the air one breathes. A contact with nature, the past, tradition." I have fallen in love with Venice, and my love for this city has become a kind of illness, a sort of sweet and calming madness. Venice has become my final anchorage: every trip into the world has a magnificent finale in the perpetual return to Venice. To leave means above all to return, and Venice's seductiveness inspires the most faithful passion.

Whether approaching by plane over the lagoon's subtly blending colors, or by train across the bridge that fragilely connects the city to the mainland, returning to Venice is always a powerful experience. The miracle is always the same—and always new.

But the most magical approach to Venice remains its most natural one: from the sea that gave the city birth and over which the city rules. The traveler who comes from the Adriatic enters Venice's most spectacular theater, the dock at Saint Mark's. The ribbon of palaces and homes is revealed from a new and utterly unique perspective, demanding that one must approach Venice by sea.

"One couldn't tell where the land ended and the water began, what was still a place or already a ship," Elstir says in *A l'ombre des jeunes filles en fleurs*.

Constructed between water, land, and sky, Venice is a magnificent exception to every architectural precept. No line is truly straight here; clocktowers lean; pavements undulate; facades shimmer. Statues have souls and surely take off on private wanderings at night, only to return to their pedestals in time for their time-honored rendezvous with tourists, streetsweepers, and pigeons.

In this city of palaces, the palaces look wobbly, as if propping each other up. Or perhaps they are trading secrets, telling each other stories, murmuring nostalgic memories. Venice is made up of dialogues in stone, compared to which words seem empty. Nothing in Venice is natural, everything is built, constructed, preserved—and everything appears obvious. The most spectacular sights seem obvious. Water is everywhere, reflecting a beauty that contemplates itself, feigning indifference toward the world's business. Light changes continually, creating beautiful vistas as if sprung from the imagination of a brilliant painter.

To live in Venice is to live in a vast, motionless, and quivering ship. Daily life is ruled by the weather's whims, and the wind is a palpable being. The scirocco is like a figure in a painting—it is the real protagonist of Guardi's and Turner's canvases. The wind sires the *acqua alta* that invades the city every winter, obliging the Venetians to wear boots all day long once they leave their homes. The wind colludes in the curious miracle that—only here—weds calamity and pleasure.

As it is everywhere, the weather is the favorite topic of conversation when Venetians meet in the great drawing room that is their city. Everyone plays a unique part: gondolier, professor, shopkeeper, or heir to a resonant family name. Inevitably, they meet in the street or in a square, pause for a moment's conversation, then go on their way. There is no point in making complicated appointments; all you have to do is go out and walk a bit, and the world comes to you.

When my children were small, I often ran into

Venice is a city of reflections and illusions . . . . At the home of the owner of Fortuny fabrics, an ancient carafe etched with a gold crown seems to multiply between a chandelier's glass pendants.

someone who would tell me about them: "I just saw Giovanni with a bandage on his knee. The pharmacist took care of him." Or, "Almoro is playing soccer with the kids in campo Santo Stefano." These encounters are so natural in Venetian life that it is not unusual to accompany a lady just met for a coffee, leading to more meetings, more casual or passionate exchanges.

But who are the Venetians, really? To be sure, many foreigners live here, but that was already true in Shakespeare's time, when he alluded to the privileges of the *forestieri*.

As Mary McCarthy observed, through the centuries Venetians have always been seen as courteous—even somewhat ceremonious—witty, and ironic. They are diplomatic, with a pronounced taste for intrigue, which they have raised to an art. In short, as Paolo Sarpi, the sixteenth-century historian notes, Venetians tell "no lies, but not everyone the truth."

Finally, though, what is this art of living in Venice? I would answer, with Rilke, "To be in Venice . . . to kneel in a church at vespers, to idle on the Zattere, to stroll down the better-known *calli* so as to run into you, to see the rose-colored house from afar. . . ."

I would add: to wander and breathe the singular rhythm of the narrow alleys that open onto broad *campi*, for Venice is music above all; to explore my favorite neighborhoods Cannaregio and Castello, for Venice is discovery and mystery; or to sit in the sun by a canal, my spirit free and at peace. Or—as I did one day with a poet friend—to wander aimlessly through the maze of streets, to get lost on purpose and discover a marble well, a doorway crowned with a coat of arms, a window hidden behind greenery, a tiny secret courtyard, a new canal. Or to slip into the silent night on a *sandalo*, the steady rhythm of the oar reverberating across the dark water.

An art to living in Venice! What a strange and obvious title. No other city has raised to such a degree of perfection this art—of happiness and of loving, of dying and of living.

Maria Teresa Rubin de Cervin

The inlaid rose windows of the Renaissance facade of Ca' Dario on the Grand Canal are mute echoes of the moon that shines over the city.

Last winter, I lived in a small apartment on the ground floor—rather, the canal floor—of the palazzetto Pisani. Gondolas grazed my windows. The *vaporetti* passed farther out, in order to pick up passengers at the Accademia bridge stop on the other side of the Grand Canal. Across from me, I could pick out the surprising romantic mosaics of palazzo Barbarigo, and the peaceful campo San Vio, which conjures up a different Venice for me, a provincial, whispering Venice, the one I love best of all. Naturally, I often ran into my landlady, the Countess Maria Pia Ferri, who lived upstairs from me and had inherited this lovely palace, with its eighteenth-century facade, from an uncle descended from the Pisani. She herself had moved to Venice with her children during the war.

"You see," she said one day, "I was afraid of the bombings, and I thought that Venice surely couldn't be bombed, not with all it represents. . . ." With a gesture, she indicated the decorated ceiling beams and the Pisani family portraits and mementos on the walls of the *piano nobile*—the "noble," or second, floor—drawing room where we sat. Beyond the windows lay the Grand Canal; the Gothic, Byzantine, and Renaissance palaces; the sublime Ca' Dario; the church of the Salute; San Giorgio Maggiore; Saint Mark's Square. Venice, all of Venice, that mirage of pure beauty. She indicated all that without a word. Why bother, when we understood each other. A gesture, silence, then she spoke again in a very soft voice, very confident of its effect: "Or, if Venice were to be bombed, it would have meant without any doubt the end of a civilization, ours, and life would no longer have been worth living." Venice wasn't bombed, and life in Venice (and therefore life itself) is still worth living. But what *is* so special about life by the Grand Canal?

During that same winter sojourn, I also met the

TO LIVE
IN VENICE

Venice, seen from one of the traghetti—like that of San Tomà (far left)—that ferry pedestrians across the Grand Canal, or from the deck of a vaporetto, amazes with its succession of Byzantine, Gothic, Renaissance, and Neoclassic facades. The city's luminosity—of water and sky, of white Istrian stone, of the marbles and colored pargeting of its houses, of its bridges—is pure, implausible, and overwhelming. Many houses are accessible by private bridges like this one, alongside the church of the Frari (above).

people who lived on the top floor of the *palazzetto*, and we became friends. The gentleman was a former senator and member of the European parliament. In his youth, he had been aide de camp to King Umberto II, who reigned for barely a month in 1946. A handsome Brittany spaniel named Sol shared the apartment with the senator and his wife. Almost every day I passed master and dog in campo San Stefano. But sometimes the dog craved solitude and independence: he loved the Dorsoduro neighborhood. He would go off alone to Santa Maria del Giglio to take the *traghetto*, the ferry that crossed there, to the shores of the promised land. The gondoliers knew him and let him on board with pleasure. In the evening, Sol stood in line like the honest Venetian he is, once more boarded the *traghetto* gondola, and returned to the Pisani *ramo*. I would hear him bark. His owners would hear him, too, and buzz the downstairs door open. Every week, the senator would ask the gondoliers how often Sol had crossed, then scrupulously pay the three-hundred-lire fare for each trip.

Life in Venice, the art of living in Venice. . . . I don't know exactly why, but I immediately think of that spaniel taking the Santa Maria del Giglio *traghetto* to Dorsoduro because he was happy in Dorsoduro. I think of a city without cars, where dogs can dawdle, snuffing the wind; where everyone knows everyone else; where lions have wings; where cats and pigeons ignore one another; where people grow accustomed to living in a kind of sphere of absolute beauty, as if all of this were natural, whereas there is nothing at all natural about Venice.

Venice is associated with sunshine for all and honeymoons for two; with carnival entertainments; and one-week guided tours going door-to-door, including a visit to the Doges' Palace, a gondola ride, and a run past the paintings in the Accademia. People will say that it is a city where one loves, lounges, admires, meditates, and dons disguises, where one is allowed to forget the great, traffic-deafened cities, but remain concerned about pollution's stealthy encroachments. The art of living in Venice—it seems too simple to write, as if it were self-evident. Yet it is the last thing non-Venetians think about. Perhaps it is unimaginable. Though Venice has inspired countless artists and writers over the centuries, their catalogue of images and impressions has overshadowed the simple fact that Venice is a city where one lives.

Aristocrats enjoy idleness here with skeptical wisdom—or else dissipation with weary elegance. Gondoliers patiently pole against time and tide. On the Mercerie, shrewd and sedentary shopkeepers contemplate the rushing crowds of day-trippers channeled inevitably into the cul-de-sac of San Marco and the Piazzetta. The island of Murano offers more than just colored-glass knickknacks: in 1290, Venice, to guard against the threat of fire, transferred its "fire trades" there. Since then, generations of glassmakers and master-glassmakers have worked on Murano. For the Venetians, Venice is not a city of transit but of habit. The city sets the pace for their leisure, their tasks, their efforts, and their hopes. They—and we—do not imagine for an instant that one may live here as one lives elsewhere, and especially not that one may live here inconsequently.

Historians have pointed out the many innovations devised by the Serenissima over the centuries, among them capitalism, the income tax, public debt and financing, and organized tourism. In addition, Venice was first to perfect an intelligence service, complete with secret agents and informers. However, historians fail to point out that Venice—cynical, commercial, violent, scheming, all-powerful, imperialist, ultra-wealthy, and the medieval capital of the world—also invented the art of living.

It is a difficult art to define precisely. Perhaps it

There is sumptuous Venice and an everyday Venice of court-yards, alleys, passageways, and earthbound pigeons. The latter is the Venice that belongs to elderly residents enjoying the fine weather in the shadow of the campo San Giovanni in Bragora. In the quiet Dorsoduro neighborhood, a glassmaking workshop is visible behind a transparent partition at the back of a courtyard (above).

evolved as Venetians balanced the reality of everyday life against the city's pure artifice. Artifice lies within this impossible city that defies all human prudence, all geographical imperatives, all reasonable limits. It is a labyrinthine city, in which one loses all one's bearings forever, a city of the maddest sensuality, the most discreet violence, the most secret opulence, and the most theatrical modesty. It is a city of whispers, the most lyrical of silent cities, a city where everything is logical—but it is the logic of dreams blossoming into the most exquisite and gratuitous conventions. It is a city that has been described, painted, sung, orchestrated, etched, rhymed, filmed, and invented a thousand times, all because it eludes definition.

Venice is not determined by a single element: it is neither an earth city like Siena, nor a standing, skyward city like New York, nor a water city like Amsterdam, but a city established in the very place where earth and water wed. It is a city that appears as suddenly as an architectural folly, defying the lagoon's menacing irresolution. The image is striking: millions and millions of oak trees sunk, whole forests ravaged, to create acres of landfill to support houses, performance halls, palaces, and churches built on these primordial mudflats. To secure its foundations and somehow consolidate its existence, the city had to find an even firmer support—the extraordinary human genius that decides to give life to its imaginings.

The word "artifice" contains the word "art," and art is everywhere in Venice, on the Grand Canal and on the tiniest *rio*, on piazza San Marco and on a *campiello*. It is in the Gothic and Oriental splendor of its palaces and in the balance, the harmony of shapes and colors of the humblest fisherfolks' home lost out on some island of the lagoon. It is in the wasted detail of a statue at the back of a forgotten Torcello garden, and in the majestic perspectives of the Salute and San Giorgio Maggiore. It is in the giddy panoply of

Tintoretto's visionary frescoes in the Scuola di San Rocco, in the modesty of a Tiepolo Virgin, or more simply still in the beauty of a gondola, a glimmer on the water, a piece of ironwork, a door-knocker, a *sotto portico* that takes you toward the unknown, toward happiness—for, in Venice, the two are always the same. Art is so pervasive that the hurried tourist or overeager visitor becomes discouraged. One gets lost in Venice, in its maze of streets, bridges, and *calli*. But above all, one gets lost in its beauty. There is nothing to remind a stranger of the common run of ugliness and wrong notes. Again, Venice is a miracle—a pure harmony of colors, lights, and reverberations. Art is everywhere, beginning with the most secret, the most delicate, the most unexpected of all: the art of living.

There are urban centers that are too cramped, where people jostle one another. There are megalopolises that are suffocating, where humanity loses sight of itself. Venetians can lose and find themselves as they please, go on foot (or by boat) anywhere in the city, greet friends, or pretend not to see them—a social art that only an advanced civilization achieves.

At the turn of the century, the Count M., who spent the better part of his days in leisure, was accustomed, every morning as he dressed, to put a handful of large beans into his right-hand jacket pocket. During the course of the day, he would pass a bean from his right pocket to his left every time he ran into a friend in the street and engaged in conversation. That evening, at home, he would count the number of beans in his left-hand pocket—seven, ten, fifteen?—to see if his day had been rich in friendship.

The Serenissima's most aristocratic cats have sometimes adopted the great families and ancient palaces. This one lies between two embroidered linen cushions on an eighteenth-century Venetian bed. Invitations hang from the knob of a marquetry door (opposite, top left). A terra-cotta bust stands out against graceful eighteenth-century stuccowork in the Balbi-Valier palace (opposite, right). The sheet music on a chair in an apartment in the Giustiniani palace (opposite, bottom left) could be that of Vivaldi, his legacy to the centuries of fascination with Venice. His was the age when the art of living reached its most intense heights of refinement. (Following pages) Giudecca and the Palladian church of the Redentore seen from the Zattere— Venice suddenly stretches into a single line, a fragile miracle between sky and water.

That's what I call the art of living, singularly revealing of a Venetian spirit very far from the conventional image popularized in the nineteenth century. Then, the Serenissima was the promised land of romantics, elegists, desperate lovers, explorers of the past, and the inconsolable for whom time had stopped. Chateaubriand best expressed that Venice, when he wrote in *Les Mémoires d'outre-tombe* in 1833: "There is enough civilization in Venice for existence to find its refinements. The heavens' seductiveness precludes the need for greater human dignity; an attracting virtue rises from these vestiges of grandeur, these traces of the arts that surround one. The wreckage of an earlier society that produced such things inspires distaste for a new society, leaving one with no desire for a future."

But the Venice of run-down palaces, half-starved cats, black-water canals, moss-eaten stones, twilight loves, and past splendors is today something of a commonplace. Venice, however, is an uncommon place, and that is a very different thing. I understand the writer Giorgio Bassani very well when he exclaims: "No, Venice is no motionless and sclerotic castle of beauty and death, but something that lives and throbs, like everything that belongs to the painful and joyous history of humanity."

A final anecdote. It is four o'clock in the morning. A foreigner asks a Venetian the way back to his hotel. The man thinks for a moment, then replies: "The fastest or the most beautiful?"

Happy the city that can inspire in one of its inhabitants so extraordinarily wise—or patient—an answer!

Frédéric Vitoux
May 1990

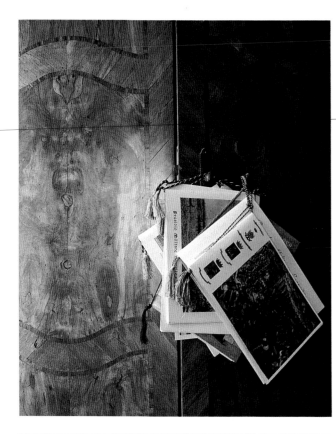

The
LAGOON

Surrounding Venice is the lagoon. More than three hundred square miles, encasing the Serenissima like a half-moon-shaped jewel box, the lagoon moves, undulates, murmurs, and effects secret metamorphoses. A soaring feeling of boundlessness seems to rise from the surface of the waters. That is what moves me, what soothes me, at first sight, this feeling inspired by a still-undetermined world, where the scents that float are at once grassy, marshy, fresh, and briny; scents I like to associate with the first days of the creation of the world. Sky, earth, fresh water, salt water—nothing seems to be fixed yet, set apart, or paralyzed within too-sharp colors or outlines. That is to say, before taking shape, the lagoon takes light. Immediately I think of Giovanni Bellini, the first of the great painters of Venice, whose paintings vibrate precisely with a simple, radiant, and innocent luminosity.

The flow of rivers and canals mingles with the wash of the sea, with the slow movement of the Adriatic tides, checked by peninsulas and sandbanks. The *barene*, those stretches that are now submerged, now emerging, sometimes appear to twinkle on the horizon below their fringes of reeds. The mysterious play of the currents, in a slow process of undermining, eroding, and filling, shifts the deepest basins and brimming lands, providential pastures for crab, shrimp, shellfish, octopus, squid, gulls, snipe, herons, wild ducks, shoveler ducks—all the incorrigible hunters and fishers. And I thought this was an inanimate realm. What a mistake! Life is everywhere here, teeming, secret, primitive beneath the sky's pale azure, where a paralyzing heart seems to solidify the water before the dusk's mercy. The lagoon—in this it is like a desert—transforms all life, every distant vision, into a mirage. It creates extraordinary enlargements. An island, a tree, a bird on a sandbank take on disproportionate importance. A campanile seems to burst from the water like a miracle from the birth of

A colored gondola, a gondola in raspberry or mauve (preceding page)? Such a thing is unimaginable in Venice: for two hundred years—since the promulgation of sumptuary laws intended to keep aristocrats from ruining themselves embellishing their boats— they have had to be entirely black. Decorated gondolas are common on the lagoon, however; they may belong to a nautical club, whose colors, like Thoroughbreds or racing cars, they sport. Sometimes you spot them and their rowers in training in this undifferentiated world, where water, land, and sky become one. Only the bricole *(opposite), the posts that mark out the lagoon's navigable channels, and the stakes that demarcate the fish-breeding areas are slight reminders of a human presence.*

the world. The lagoon is not a real landscape—it is a landscape of dreams.

It is always difficult to live in a dream. One has first to domesticate it and then to give it order. And this human order that reigns over the lagoon is symbolized by the *bricole*, those posts driven into the mud which mark the navigable channels and which form a grid over a borderless landscape and endow its sweetness, its tenderness, its boundless and magical beauty with a sense of geometry—that is, of reason.

To divine the secret, the genius of Venice and its citizens, you must let yourself be affected by this landscape. You must imagine for a moment its earliest inhabitants, who gathered salt there, sought there a defensible place, a place of survival and freedom, safe form the barbarians . . . this is what provides the incomparable key to it. The lagoon allows one to understand, or rather, to partake of the sweetness of Venetian living, the nonchalant patience of the inhabitants, and the calm, musical quality of a language that shies from double consonants and too-marked tonic accents. There is an incredible inventive genius in the way Venetians love, trade, or marvel at practically anything—particularly the lagoon, one of Venice's most hidden secrets because it offers itself artlessly to too-distracted glances.

The geographers are quick to point out the "ecological miracle" represented by the lagoon, a fragile equilibrium between the elements that it comprises, with an average depth of around two feet. They distinguish the *laguna viva*, more subject to the influences of the sea and the tides, from the *laguna morta*, sunk deep into the *valli*, into solid ground, and which sometimes assumes the appearance of an inanimate marsh. Then there are the surveyors, the historians who expatiate on the lagoon and go into raptures, for example, over the Serenissima's efforts, in the eighteenth century, to build the famous *murazzi* of Istrian stone from Sottomarina to the Lido—a "great wall of

China," meant to protect the lagoon from the sea's assaults. But I prefer, to the geographers, or the surveyors, or the historians—Venice's true lovers—the countryfolk, the naturalists, the dreamers, the aesthetes, the fisherfolk, and even the hunters who live on the lagoon, or rather, by the lagoon.

An entire fish-breeding economy has been established in the *valli da pesca* by means of a fairly complex system of dams, barrages, and filters. In the valley, eels are hatched and bred, along with *branzini* (sea bass), *cefali* (gray mullet) and *orate* (gilthead). In contrast to the *valli de pesca* are the *valli da caccia*, located predominantly between Venice and Chioggia. Often purchased by wealthy owners from Milan, Mestre, and Bologna, these are, in autumn and winter, the paradise of duck-hunters who lease the right to lie in ambush before dawn, in a sort of barrel, a *botte*. There they await their prey, confident of bagging their game. I feel a greater affinity with the more peaceable strollers of a *valle* like the Valle dell' Averto, which is managed by the World Wildlife Foundation. There, buffalo chew their cud, turkeys strut, and the observation platforms above the rushes allow one to admire—not slaughter—herons, ducks, egrets, swans, dragonflies, mosquitoes, and all else that enjoys the refuge.

In the lagoon, the water is so mirror-like one can watch the clouds go by in it, so limpid, one can follow the fishes' silvery trails—a thrilling (or unbearably frustrating) game for a gun-dog at point, an unlikely figurehead at the prow of his boat.

Many of the lagoon's meanders are given over to fish-breeding—the Venetians call them valli da pesca. What a difference between this forgotten, primitive world, with its shanties, its sheds for fishing nets, its expanses of marsh—those splendid natural defenses that have always pro-tected the city from invaders—and the extraordinary luxury of the Serenissima a few miles away! In the season when the soft-shelled crabs of which the Venetians are so fond shed their carapaces, they are taken to mar-ket in nets submerged at the boats' sides.

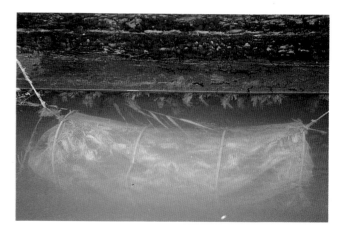

The valli da pesca *and* valli da caccia—*the latter reserved for hunting—overlap narrowly in the lagoon's labyrinthine twists and turns.*

The lagoon offers itself, passive, indolent, fascinating, amniotic, and hypnotic. But the great, inert, and docile body awakens savage passions and rouses superhuman efforts and endless quarrels. The Venetians are a people of compromises, nuances, deals, diplomatic subtleties, murmured words, and indulgent opinions. They are doubting, tolerant, not very religious, not very quick-tempered—as long as no one mentions the lagoon. Then their passions are instantly aroused and their intransigence explodes.

One evening, a half dozen friends dined in a small apartment on the top floor of an old house in the campo San Polo. We spoke of Bonaparte, of Venice, of the citizens who fled their city, and the tourists who invaded it, of *Madame Butterfly*, which was playing at La Fenice, and of the World's Fair of the year 2000, for which Venice had bid. During dessert, the conversation dwindled, despite the excellent pastries and our hostess's liveliness. I said the word "lagoon," and, across from me, an architect about fifty years old, with a salt and pepper beard and of a somewhat ecological bent, leapt up. He had seemed to me a gentle Samaritan— suddenly he became Savonarola. He seized the conversation and didn't give it back all evening. He held us spellbound with his vision of the lagoon. He grabbed large pieces of paper to sketch illustrations and demonstrations. His passion spiraled

On the lagoon, the sheds that house the boats and the workshops where the fishing nets dry are more precious even than peoples' homes. A strange feeling of peace reigns in these places, a chiaroscuro that is almost eerie beside the lagoon's pure, steady light. Under the Madonna's protection, a fish-hatchery worker changes his clothes as a priest does his vestments.

and spread, possessing us all in its vital frenzy.

Would Venice sink into the ground? Not at all, he replied to our brief and infrequent interventions. That problem was under control, as was the problem of pollution in the atmosphere! And would the sea level rise, due to the worldwide phenomenon that the physicists call the "greenhouse effect"? That was worrisome, certainly. But he reserved his arguments for more specific targets. He described those ships of increasingly gigantic tonnage that were sweeping by the city, causing the channels to be dredged constantly to facilitate passage to Marghera. That let more and more seawater into the lagoon. He showed us how the tides' faster and more violent waves weakened Venice, altered the relief of the lagoon bottom, destroyed the shellfish, and impeded the water's regeneration.

Certain industrialists have proposed a spectacular

The brick landing-stage of the cason Zappa (above), situated in the middle of one of the lagoon's most beautiful valli—just like the casone of this valle, the vacation and hunting property of a Venetian noble family (left). To the north, the Alps rise, rose-colored and ghostly.

and onerous remedy: the construction of a movable underwater barrage, to be set in place during the spring tides in order to minimize their damage to the lagoon and to the city. The plan seemed to him a ruinous joke. Who would decide to raise the dikes of the barrage, and when? No, that was out of the question, but it would be so easy to reduce the activity of the port, install platforms out at sea, and lay pipelines to take the oil to the refineries.

We finally left our friends' apartment at five in the morning. The campo San Polo was empty. The pigeons had long been sleeping and the cats were pursuing their tumultuous love lives elsewhere. The tourists were out of sight, no doubt regaining their strength in order to face the hurly-burly at Saint Mark's later that morning. The ecologist-architect said good night to us with affection tinged with regret.

"I haven't explained anything yet, anything at all. Call me tomorrow, come by my office, I can give you more details about the real problems in the lagoon!"

Are the Venetians great navigators? A remark by Malaparte, the Tuscan master of paradoxes and provocations, comes to mind: "The Venetians were not seafarers: they were country folk accustomed to wrenching their bit of land from the swamp. A country person has a field outside the door, not a square. Hence the word *campo* or field by which the Venetians call their squares. They come out onto their squares as country folk go into their fields; to look at the sky, the outdoors, space. From deep in their ancient memory, the square recalls fields, countryside, trees. Canals remind them of ditches, so they call a canal a *rio*, the word for ditch in the villages of Venezia. The Venetians call the dead-end alleyways *rami*—branches—because they resemble the dead branches of trees. Branches of the ancient forest that live on, deep in their memory. The Venetians call a certain kind of narrow street *salzada*, in memory of willow-lined paths. Even the word *corte* is used to describe not a courtyard but a certain space contrived between houses, recalling the yards in the villages of the Venezia countryside. . . ."

Nevertheless, these former country folk have made the lagoon their playground, fairground, and exercise ground. Those who live on the islands and the dunes, on Malamocco or Chioggia, have in fact become true sailors—with all due respect to Malaparte. But every-

There are many nautical clubs in Venice, like the Bucintoro on the Zattere, where one may learn to row Venetian-style. Above the picture of the Bucentaur hang the forcole that lock the oars on the sides of the boats (opposite, bottom left). Some racing clubs have taken over the old slaughterhouses of Venice, in the Canareggio sestiere, to serve as their headquarters. There they can house their boats, whose flat bottoms, and therefore shallow draft, allow them to venture onto areas of the lagoon where the ground almost meets the water's surface.

one, be they from Dorsoduro or Burano, San Marco or Vignole, for any reason or no reason at all, for an hour of relaxation or an afternoon away from the city and their professional concerns, takes out a boat and starts to row.

My friend Paolo, who lives near the Arsenale, confided in me one day something that he finds amusing. His neighbor, a grocer, takes his boat out at dawn every day of the week to get stock for his store or to make deliveries. Yet on the weekends he can imagine nothing more enjoyable than to get back into his boat and take his family for a picnic on one or another island. People row in Venice and on the lagoon, my friend said, for the same reasons others jog in the streets of great metropolises crowded with cars, pedestrians, dust, and gas smells.

The idols of the Venetians are not soccer players or boxers, but rowers, champions of their clubs on the Dogana, Giudecca, Burano, on every island. They compete and challenge each other over nothing, any event will do, and the events are many. For parties in Venice are always water parties.

I remember the September *Regata storica*. The parade barges are taken out, along with the gondolas saved for special occasions, and the gaudiest costumes. The canals shimmer with a thousand colors. All the clichés come true. History stands still—or a gentle caricature of history. Every craft is more beautiful than the one before.

For the feast of the Redentore, the third Sunday in July, a veritable bridge of boats forms from the Zattere to Giudecca, specifically, to the Palladian church of the Redentore, built to mark the end of the great plague of 1576. Once again, Venice is afloat. It is a contest to see who can best decorate their boats with leaves, flowers, and lanterns. Everyone finds the best spots from which to admire the fireworks over the Saint Mark's basin. Everyone dines on board, on terraces, on balconies, everywhere. Roast duck, *sar-*

dine in saor, pasta, beans, and the fish dish characteristic of Giudecca. The *prosecco frizzante* flows like water. Venice keeps its past alive—its traditions are its current events as well. And when the last flares have been shot into the sky and the last bottles emptied into glasses, then the boats massed by Giudecca turn toward the Lido, where the Venetians will wait on the beach for sunrise. But so many boats together make me mildly suspicious. It is as if they were erasing the water by their numbers, as if they were in some way filling the canals. This is no longer boating—you could almost walk around from boat to boat, unaware of islands, tide, everything.

There is no ambiguity in the *Vogalonga*, the popular sporting event created in 1975. It is to Venice and its lagoon what the marathon has become to New York City. All you need is a craft of some kind, and the ability to row. On the first Sunday after the Ascension, hundreds take off from the Saint Mark's basin for an exhausting circuit more than eighteen miles long. They round Sant' Elena, touch at San Erasmo, hug Burano and Torcello, return by way of Murano, and take the Cannaregio canal to enter the Grand Canal and finish between Saint Mark's and the Dogana. Some row to win; some row to row; some row because rowing is fundamental to living in Venice and being happy in Venice. Here, one rows as one breathes, for the beauty of the gesture, intimacy with the lagoon, the secret pleasure of the effort, and the satisfaction of saying, "I did it!"

"You can't imagine the Vogalonga," I was told by a Venetian lady who has the *piano nobile* of a palace whose water door opens onto the rio dei Frari. She lives quietly with her cat and her son and she crochets. But sometimes at dusk she rows alone, to enter into a sort of silent complicity with her city. At nine in the morning all the bells chime, sirens and alarms sound. The fire fighters flourish their fire hoses over the Saint Mark's basin. You hold your oar straight

The Vogalonga *departs (above) from the Saint Mark's dock, across from San Giorgio Maggiore, the first Sunday after Ascension Day. Firefighters flourish their firehoses. Contestants—amateur and accomplished athletes, lovely "daughers of the lagoon" in beflowered boats, and veteran Venetians in the traditional red-and-white-striped jerseys—prepare for a "marathon" that will take them the length of San Erasmo, around Burano, Torcello, and Murano, and finally back to Venice.*

up—the ancient salute to Venice and the Republic—and you take off. A four-hour effort at least, and sometimes currents so strong that it becomes almost impossible to go forward. The most bizarre craft pass you: Norwegian long ships, Tahitian pirogues, and the oldest boats on the lagoon. And the way back! On the Cannaregio canal, the party is at its peak, people are there waiting to applaud for us. People even put bathmats out their windows for decoration. They bang pot covers. Finally, the arrival at the Dogana. What time is it, one or two in the afternoon? You don't know anymore, you can't go on. Hands and legs are exhausted. I've done two Vogalonga with my son, and five alone on board my *mascareta*. Unforgettable."

The lagoon doesn't just prowl around Venice, it infiltrates it. Its tides set the rhythm of the city's breathing. Sometimes the lagoon threatens the city with disturbing levels of the *acqua alta*. And of all the boats on the lagoon, one kind has multiplied in Venice to the point of becoming its reference and absolute symbol—the gondola.

Why its funereal color? Some say it is because the sumptuary laws enacted three hundred years ago forbade the always-too-prodigal Venetians to paint and decorate their boats. I prefer to believe that black is the homage that Venice renders to the limitless azure of the sky, the sapphire blue or gray-green of the canals, the enchanting luminosity of its Gothic and Byzantine palaces. One does not compete with such a palette. The gondola prefers, so to speak, to keep to the pure perfection of its outlines, a spare, slender, airy aesthetic derived from its functionality alone (except for the six metal teeth at the prow, which probably refer to the six areas, or *sestieri*, of the city).

Its slight dissymmetry maintains the equilibrium between the gondolier's weight and the thrust of the oar. No other craft needs so little water to float, nor can pivot on itself so gracefully despite its thirty-three-foot length, nor can reach such speeds transporting so many passengers. A gondola is made of 280 pieces of walnut, hazel, oak, beech, mahogany, linden, larch, and cherrywood. It remains Venice's finest invention.

"A gondola is a sweet interval of pleasure," wrote an eighteenth-century French traveler. I dare not regret too openly the Serenissima's bygone ways, the times of Carnival, courtesans, endless games of love and chance. But I have no compunction about deploring the disappearance from the gondola of the *felze*—that providential shelter from the rigors of the climate and the indiscreet curiosity of strangers. With its curved roof, sliding windows, and painted-wood panels, the *felze* resembled an aquatic carriage. They were still to be seen at the turn of the century. Alas! None of the patrician families still has its own gondola—nor its own gondolier, who, in the latter days of his reign, also acted as odd-job man at the palazzo. Those crafts are captured in Guardi's or Canaletto's *vedute*, or in sepia photographs in old family albums.

The gondola is not the only vehicle to appear on the Grand Canal or to prosper on the lagoon. Other boats proliferate there. And just as a zoologist is careful not to mistake, for example, a ferruginous duck for a Muskovy duck, or a pochard for an eider, so will navigators of the lagoon distinguish, at first glance, the *mascareta*—very widespread today because it is light and relatively inexpensive to produce—from the *batela bruranela*, which is fast and easy to handle, even though it is used for work and transportation, or the *cofano*, very much favored by hunters lying in wait, from the *sciopon*, once used to track the passage of migratory birds and bring them down with a blunderbuss. Although the *sanpierota* is used exclusively for fishing, the *topo* is still the most popular barge. The famous *caorlina* that we find in many sixteenth-century etchings is still in fine fettle and mettle in the *Regata storica*, representing the is-

The Burano boatyards are among the best in Venice, and on the lagoon—at least in the opinion of the residents of Burano, who also consider themselves the best rowers. In any case, this armchair for a gondola (top), richly decorated for a wedding, is indisputably wonderful, as are the gondoliers' elegance and virtuosity in handling their crafts and the colors of boats beached or poised upon the water as lightly as seabirds.

lands of the lagoon. Each *caorlina* displays the colors of its island, and is decorated with allegories that illustrate that island's traditional activities.

Are some of these species becoming extinct? The *motoscafi* of the nouveaux riches, the outboards, and the vaporetti, all these backfiring combustion craft certainly jeopardize them. The newcomers to the canal disturb the water, the fish's tranquility, the philosopher's meditation, and the fisherman's siesta. Besides, it is impossible for a boat with a propeller to meander where it likes on the lagoon, to graze the *barene*, to manage in a few inches of water to float, move, breathe, slip around, commune with nature, and admire the sky reflected in the mirror of the sea.

I remember a stroll on the lagoon one autumn day recently. The sun could not quite break through the fog that floated monotonous and far above our heads. The vegetation was the color of verdigris, the water had the gray-blue glimmers of steel. We barely dared to speak. The least sound would have ripped through the muffled harmony of the world and started time in motion once more.

After rounding the Giardini and Sant' Elena, after passing and forgetting the few dismal islands used today as warehouses or drill grounds for the Italian naval forces (what threat are they guarding against? what invaders do they eternally await—Turks, Tartars, Genoese, Russians, Libyans, extraterrestrials?), we skirted the Vignole. Small sandstone houses were girdled with vegetable gardens.

In this unexpected scene of petit bourgeois harmony Venice forgot all its splendor, all thirst for conquest. A path ran along the canal. We came upon a wedding. The bridal couple, their family, and friends were in procession toward a modest chapel whose facade was losing its pargeting in patches. We waved to the bride from afar. She waved back. The bridegroom was smiling at his future wife, at the strangers who waved, at the milky sky, at the quacking ducks, at

Venice, and at the future. An artless happiness reigned over this suburban Cythera so near to and so far from the pomp and crowds of Saint Mark's Square. The newlyweds on the lagoon lived light-years from all that. In fact, that morning they were living in a world without any light at all, that is, without contrasting colors. They were living in a black and white world, the bride's white, the groom's black suit, the cream color of the sky, the water's grays, a muffled world, but whether liquid or solid, one couldn't tell. A world that had rightly chosen to enclose itself within a parenthesis of life. Then our boat left the wedding behind, left the Vignole for the shores of San Erasmo. Suddenly the sun broke through the fog. The clocks started up again. The couple must have already said the fateful "I do." Reeds tossed on the horizon, gulls took flight as we approached, and we heard the sound of oars.

There was color and life! Two long boats (*mascarete*, perhaps) slipped on the surface of the water, each propelled by two men rowing Venetian-style: standing, faces to the wind, oars bracketed to the craft in the *forcole*, hinges that look a little like Jean Arp sculptures. Why do they row that way? The usual, prosaic answer is: because the Venice canals are narrow. The oar cannot reach too far from the boat, but must be plunged virtually perpendicular to the lagoon. I prefer to believe that it is an art that, first of all, has to do with a state of mind, a way of looking forward and divining distant dangers and the least quiverings and traps of the lagoon. How can you row turning your back to the future?

One of the boats was bright pink. The other was an emerald green. They swept around behind some *bricole* and disappeared, elegant and quick, enchanted and natural, gentle birds of the lagoon.

"*Regatanti* from a nautical club," explained the pilot of the *motoscafo* who was driving us that morning. "And do you know," he added, "who makes the best rowers,

Burano is the provincial island, cheerful and optimistic, where the facades sing like opera sets. It is the island of fisherfolk, lacemakers, and daydreamers, the hospitable island, where in summer colored canvas blinds shelter open doors from the sun's rays and the invading flies.

Burano is a riot of color, from the Fondamenta della Pescheria, where the fishing boats dock, to the back of a courtyard near the Corte Comare, to homes adorned with curious corner balconies of wrought iron. In fact, Burano's colors obey strict rules: the fronts of houses must be repainted every year because the humidity fades them. The shade may not be changed—a yellow house must remain yellow. Two adjoining houses may not be the same color. In contrast, the lacemakers bring time to a standstill with their immaculate white handiwork.

Whether or not the Lido is still Europe's most elegant resort, come June it is time to rake the sand, ready the beach, and repaint the tentpoles that support the summer living rooms of Venetian families. The crowds will certainly arrive, putting to flight the scattering of nuns who sometimes venture here off season.

the best gondoliers?"

We didn't know.

"People from Burano, of course, because, in the old days, to go to work in Venice, they had to row a long way every day."

We asked where he was from. "Burano," he said.

We left San Erasmo, its vineyards, vegetable gardens, tomato and potato farms, and its boat houses. The sun that had so suddenly appeared, retired behind a new layer of fog. It didn't matter, because we were coming up on Burano, and Burano, with its pink, green, blue, ocher, beige, and violet houses, always has rainbow colors to spare for a winter or rainy day.

From offshore, we could pick out the royal blue Antonio Amadi workshops, which make indisputably the most beautiful racing boats on all the lagoon. Farther on, at the foot of each dock, around each ladder down to the water, tiny walnut hulls congregated, their motors good only for very modest horsepower.

"Ah, the children," sighed our pilot, with a knowledgeable air. "They all want motorboats. Over there"—he indicated the mainland, the continent—"the young people have mopeds and motorcycles. Here, this is what they want, this is what they get," he said, indicating the little boats with their outboard motors. A slightly melancholy light shone in his eyes.

The Lido unquestionably belongs to Venice geographically, but less so spiritually. Once upon a time, the Lido was a no-man's-land, an endless, desolate, and sandy frontier between the sea and the lagoon. Lord Byron ran his horses there. One must always beware of poets—they set fashions. Lord Byron may still have swum alone in the lagoon, but by the late nineteenth century sea bathing was utterly chic among the middle classes around the world. From 1860 on, there sprouted on the Lido deluxe hotels, secondary residences, shady lanes, seaside villas, and motorcars. Would the neo-Moorish Excelsior or the Hotel des Bains win out as the sumptuous meeting-place of the summering elite, in a whirl of hat veils, parasols, chilly dips, tea dances, refined ennui, and languid flirtations? I confess a weakness for the rustic-cottage–style Quattro Fontane and the oft-overlooked Hungaria Hotel, a little way from the beach. The latter's pale green facade is adorned with extravagant processions of garlanded young ladies who timelessly sing the praises of the Belle Époque. There, or on the Lido's strand of fine sand, where the word "pollution" was as yet unknown, the beautiful Venetian women—their type once summarized by Gozzi as *"biondo, bianco e grassotto"*—mingled at the turn of the century with women from Austria, Hungary, and Milan, with brunette women, slender women, pale women, and tubercular women, with widows and demi-mondaines, those worldly women who did nothing by halves.

Basta! Those days are gone. The Lido that turned its back to Venice, that lived openly from the sea as if collaborating with the invaders, merely survives its past glory. Today, on a whim, we bathe in the Seychelles, tan in the Caribbean, dry off in Madagascar, and dive once more—into the green waters of Tuamotu. Still, the Venetians who haven't fled their city during the summer months find the Lido's gardens have lost none of their charm, nor the roses their

Venice captures light to sumptuous effect, like white Istrian stone that at sunset turns rosy-pink the length of the quays by the Giardini. From there, one can see the low, twinkling line of houses on Giudecca (above). Dusk in Venice is symbolized by San Michele, the island of the dead that resembles an Oriental palace, girdled by a wall of white-edged, rose-pink brick. It lies between Murano and Venice, and its triple gate—now filled in —once opened onto the Serenissima, across from the Fondamenta Nuove.

perfume, nor the pittosporums their brilliance. They consider themselves lucky indeed to rent a cabana on the fine-sand beaches that claim "No Vacancy." Those who crave golf will find their beloved greens and fairways a little farther on. In September the Film Festival revives the Lido's glamor, but only to celebrate other times, other screens, other illusions. I want to believe that the real, everyday life of Venice and its lagoon, at least the one I love, is far from the Lido.

Where? On San Lazzaro degli Armeni, whose perfectly quadrilateral shape makes the island seem abstract, where lepers were confined, and where there are still paintings by Tiepolo and Longhi? Or, at the other end of the lagoon, near Torcello, on the sublime little island of San Francesco del Deserto, dressed in cypresses that seem painted by Böcklin, and where, they say, Saint Francis rested after a stormy night? If the legend isn't true, never mind. It is still preferable to reality, especially in Venice where legend is built of stone and marble. On that island, a handful of Franciscan monks turn their thoughts to God in a thirteenth-century monastery of unparalleled sobriety, sheltered from life's weariness, false hopes, and real disillusionments, in the overwhelming silence of the lagoon. This little island could make one desire faith, never to doubt if such a thing were possible. A narrow canal plunges inland, reaching the monastery walls like a prayer granted at last.

Or is the real life of Venice found on San Michele, the Island of the Dead, between Murano and the Fondamenta Nuove? With the delicate and soothing Renaissance facade of its little church, its tall cypresses like funeral tapers, is this the same way of life found when Napoleon arbitrarily ordered the cemetery of Venice to be built here? You have to have landed on San Michele once during All Saints' Week to know. A free vaporetto takes the inhabitants of the city from the Fondamenta Nuove to the island. The women carry flowers—their figures swallowed up by

pots of huge chrysanthemums, rumpled and white, yellow, and pink. They look like an army of flowers on the march disembarking in front of the church and the Emiliani chapel, filing into the right-angle lanes of the cemetery. The chrysanthemums advance like the forest in *Macbeth*. The gaudy pots of flowers are in place in front of each tombstone. The living have done their duty. They return to the vaporetto, satisfied. Perhaps the dead are, too. To one side, in the Russian enclosure, Diaghilev's grave is lost beneath a tangle of bramble and wild rose, not far from Stravinsky's. Carved into Ezra Pound's tombstone is only his name—sans date, sans everything. What do birth and death really mean to a poet or to Venice? Life is instantaneous and eternal. San Michele lives, palpitates in its lagoon, its spring tides, its waters in which life rises from decay. San Michele, between Venice and Murano, does not speak to us of death, but of a very temporary halt to the happiness of living.

In a room of the Doges' Palace, there is a 1516 painting by Carpaccio that represents *The Lion of Saint Mark*. In the background are the *piazzetta* and the Doges' Palace. On the left, also in the background, is a Venetian fleet setting sail, no doubt to conquer new ports and new markets. The winged animal rests its two front paws on a desolate mainland; its two hind paws still rest on the water. Though this may symbolize a new Venetian triumph on foreign soil, I see it above all as a perfect summary of the city. Two feet on the water, two feet on land, wings to conquer the sky. The Lion of Venice, that absolute emblem of the Serenissima, is first and foremost the lion of a lagoon that merges all its elements. Made of mud, of salty freshwater, swampland, and sandy terrains; of mother-of-pearl and opal beneath an immense sky, the lagoon offers itself like a nuptial bed in which each year was celebrated the marriage of the doge and the Adriatic in a dazzling ceremony. The lagoon is life itself to Venice. It is where the Lion of Saint Mark walks, swims, and flies.

There is no better symbol of the beauty and onetime maritime power of Venice than the Punta della Dogana, the former marine customs house crowned by two bronze telamons bearing a gilded globe (right). Behind it, on Giudecca, the silhouette of the Palladian church of the Redentore. The quay at the Zattere (below), where boats sometimes dock—like this sailboat on which a family lives year-round.

44

DECOR

I had long felt that one didn't so much live life in Venice as playact there. The city was a set, the facades of the palaces on the Grand Canal were immense folding screens, two-dimensional flats put up to impress tourists and please the Venetians who have always loved to perform in the show that is their city.

I knew this was all true because I had never, during the course of my early strolls, encountered—through shutters left ajar, an indiscreet window, or a door absently left open—a scene of domestic intimacy. No woman in her kitchen, no child by a curtain, no group of friends at a table. When the Venetians went home, they disappeared without a trace. Still, what would the Venetians do at home anyway? They already do everything outdoors—have parties, make love, cook, converse, intrigue, philosophize, perform, politick, and create. Venice gives its inhabitants, visitors, and lovers the illusion of an immense home, a house-city where one lives sheltered from the disorders, violence, accidents, and fears of the outside world.

Napoleon said Saint Mark's Square was Europe's most elegant drawing room. And so it is, with its sumptuous decor: the Byzantine basilica, its Romanesque campanile; the Gothic Doges' Palace; the Turco-Gothic-Renaissance new and old Procurators' palaces; the lymphatic pigeons; and the Roman Empire–style *logetta*. On winter nights the mist crowns the cupolas of Saint Mark's and muffles up the campanile, like dustcovers thrown over the furniture after a party. That is when I like to wander around the piazza and play with the fanciful notion that I am the host here. Then I am once again in that too-huge drawing room, that entirely artificial beauty, that giddy invention where the centuries crash to create a unique and monumental harmony where one feels marvelously comfortable.

Yet, to Saint Mark's I prefer other drawing rooms. For state occasions, for example, I like Santi Giovanni

Colonnades, galleries, porticoes . . . With its passageways, windings, and squares, Venice presents itself less as a city to be methodically explored, than as a city always full of surprises. For example, from the Punta della Dogana (above) one can see, beyond the mouth of the Grand Canal, the old Giardini Reali, which back onto the Procuratie Nuove. The refreshing shade of a covered passageway on Giudecca, near the graceful Palladian church of the Zitelle, frames another unexpected view of the Grand Canal. There are cities like this: their genius lies not only in their beauty, but in their gift for setting a stage. Proving this in the Zattere (preceding pages), near rio San Vio, this enigmatic child with an open book on a brick wall inspires wise reflections.

Is Venice a city made only of light? One could believe it from the warm, mother-of-pearl dusk over the church of the Salute and the palaces on the Grand Canal, sparkling and ablaze (following pages).

e Paolo (*San Zanipolo*, as the Venetians say). There, no matter how much the condottiere Bartolomeo Colleoni swashbuckles astride his bronze horse, clenches his teeth, frowns, and gives himself airs of a duce or a Roman emperor, he cannot impress his admirers, old relatives, courtesans—the regulars. They no longer even raise their heads to greet him, render him homage, as they come and go in his home as if they were in their own. They chat, lounge, drink an espresso at the Colleoni or the Cavallo (how wonderful that these two neighboring cafés give you the freedom to choose between the soldier and his mount!), get ready to go out—to church to ask God to keep them in health, or else to the Scuola di San Marco, the public hospital, to ask the doctors to cure them on the spot!

For elegant receptions, Santa Maria Formosa, with its delightful asymmetry, is without equal. There is always a crowd there, assessing one another, looking each other in the eye, talking of fair weather and foul. However, it is well-bred enough to ignore the grotesque mask of an abominable parasite—the *Mascaron!*—that intrudes on them, sculpted at the base of the square's Baroque campanile.

Venice is a place with a thousand corners to turn, an extravagant and labyrinthine house, with its rooms, hallways, galleries, guardrooms, staircases, attics, drawing rooms, sitting rooms, and laundry rooms. Venice encloses its inhabitants, spellbinds them, leads them astray, grabs them, surprises them, allows them no skyward escape. Only the Grand Canal dilates the city, opening it onto space. You may cross it on the Rialto or the Accademia bridge, or on board a *traghetto* (what an uneasy pleasure in being penned in with ten or twelve people standing in the middle of a gondola, briskly propelled by rowers at prow and stern, indifferent to eddies or closely passing vaporetti!), but once on the other side you plunge back into the first passage you come to.

At night this feeling of "interiority" is at its stron-

gest, which is why Venice seems to me above all a nocturnal city. I associate it with long walks at two or three in the morning, returning to my hotel or rented apartment after a dinner. Then more than ever, the *calli* resemble hallways endlessly branching off. There is no sky. There are no palaces, houses, or churches around me. There are only partitions and sometimes mirages. Footsteps echo in the distance. Other lovers are awake and walking through the same house. Will we meet? The steps are getting closer. Danger? No, there is no danger, no threat. I am at home. In Venice there are no run-ins, only encounters.

I think to live here is to live in the only city in the world where there is such a reassuring feeling of security. One does not consider for a moment that one might be attacked at the corner of the *rio*. Women walk alone at night without a thought. Jewels, ingots, rivers of diamonds can sleep as soundly in the bank vaults as in their own little beds. The "poor little rich girls" come out of school with light hearts and heavy bookbags, without swarms of bodyguards to protect them and discourage possible kidnappings. Kidnap someone in Venice? What would you use for a getaway car? Try to rob a bank and lose your pursuers without falling into a canal. No wonder the richest Milanese industrialists moved their families here during the time of the Red Brigades. Venice is an urban maze, a fortress for the joy of living, where the evildoers find it hard to escape after a crime. Or just find it hard to do evil. . . .

Everything about Venice—the proportions of its squares, courtyards, and alleyways, the harmony of its architecture, the steel blue of its night sky, the gray-green glints off its canals, the very materials from which it is built (luminous white Istrian stone, blood-red brick, polychrome marble), the greens of moss proliferating at the foot of palaces, even the mute, warm, suffering ocher of the pargeting falling off in patches—lets you believe that anything is

possible at any moment: a carnival, insouciance, the forgetting of mornings-after, love, and, more simply and prosaically, the pleasure of stopping and chatting. Once again, the pleasures of the drawing room.

On the exterior walls of palaces and houses, above windows and the lintels of doorways, sculpted heads seem to carry on a secret conversation. The majestic presence of the Lion of Venice, emblem of the Serenissima, is everywhere. ("Venice, the only city in the world where pigeons walk and lions fly," said Jean Cocteau). However, neither the heads nor the lions are at all frightening. It is unusual for a city to inspire such a quality of peace. One street a little too long, one building a little too high, one shop a little too brightly lit, one canal a little too wide, one square a little too large, one bridge a little too steep, and the

The San Polo neighborhood, seen from an altana *(opposite). The roofs, churches, and campaniles of the San Marco neighborhood; and in the distance, the basilica's bulbed cupolas (above, left). The bridge of the Accademia, discovered beyond the roofs of a palace on the Grand Canal (above, center top). Another view of the Grand Canal, beyond the terrace of palazzo Pisani-Moretta (above, center bottom). Venice's characteristic chimneys (above, right) give an unexpected picture of the Serenissima as a crowded, jostling city where the only space, the only breathing room is on the water or skyward.*

miracle wouldn't work. The Venetians would no longer feel at home in their parishes, on their *campi*, discussing the whole world, the lagoon, and their next-door neighbor's health. When the Goldoni theater near campo San Luca was rebuilt, for example, with its dull new surfaces of shiny stone and its oppressive mass, it drove the inhabitants of the area away and discouraged the cats that used to gather in the Corte del Teatro to meditate on world affairs, the madness of men, and the sweetness of life.

Venetian cats . . . there were about seventy thousand in the early 1960s, often wretched, mangy, and dying. Inspired by the untiring energy of an Englishwoman, Helena Sanders, an association named Dingo began a program of birth and population control, health care, and supervision of nutrition. After

Winged or not, emblems of the Serenissima or decorative elements, lions are as ubiquitous in Venice as cats. This lion keeps an eye on the painter Hundertwasser's garden on Giudecca from the cornice of a wall. Very 1900-style street lamps (right)— cast by Valese in Venice—on the Riva di Ca' di Dio, which extends the Riva degli Schiavoni toward the Arsenal and the Giardini.

twenty years' effort, the feline population is stable at about six thousand. Whose cats are they? They belong to no one. Cats never belong to anyone. Venice belongs to *them*. They colonized it. They alone conquered Venice, where they have established several headquarters, according to the season and their fancy. Are the cats that meditate by the Scuola di San Rocco the most philosophical? The ones that warm themselves in campo San Vidal, by the Accademia bridge, during the first fine spring days the most epicurean? Those that nibble the papyri of the little garden of the Querini-Stampalia palace the greatest gourmets? Those that play among the ruins and rank weeds of the palazzo Contarini, at the foot of the Scala del Bovolo, the most easy-going and unpredictable? I know certain cats, between San Polo and the rio della Madonnetta, who live on rooftops and thrive at that altitude. A friend of mine feeds them on her *altana*. One day, she tried to bring one of the tomcats downstairs. Crazed by the sound and fury at street level, he raced back up, four stairs at a time, and made her open all the doors between himself and the peaceful serenity of the heights, leaving his less lofty colleagues the task of chasing rats.

As I came to know Venice and learned to live there, I learned to take everything as a whole, to love everything with that absolute love that never weighs the pros and cons, the satisfactions and the disap-

Only a few meters from the Rialto, with its glitzy shops, the Venice market displays its wares. It is the city's most active, popular, and colorful spot. Sailors and merchants no longer unload their cargoes of spices, silks, or dyes from the Orient as they did here in the Middle Ages—the truck farmers of the lagoon have long since taken their place. Be-

yond the Erberia—the vegetable market—opens the Pescheria, the famous fishmarket, where gilt-heads, eels, sardines, and all the lagoon's seafood, with its pungent sea-scent, recalls the Serenissima's eternal marine calling (bottom left). But there are many other markets in the city, like that of the vast campo Santa Margherita (top right).

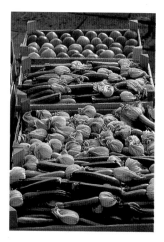

The residents of Dorsoduro have long enjoyed the last truck farmer's barge, docked along rio di San Barnaba. A large, colored canvas canopy protects it from the sun—and the pigeons.

pointments, the preferences and rejections.

In my view, that is the most amazing secret of the city: the incredible unity that it reveals in the brilliant diversity of its styles. Its earliest buildings—like the San Marco basilica and the church of San Giacomo, near the Rialto—date to the eleventh century. In the twelfth century, the Veneto-Byzantine palaces—the Ca' Loredan and the Ca' Farsetti, for example—began to multiply, with their great entrance halls, their porticos opening onto the canal to receive merchandise, and the vast central gallery that bisects the *piano nobile*. Venetian Gothic blossomed in the fourteenth and into the fifteenth centuries, leaving its lasting mark on the city. Palaces kept the same structure, but windows became ogival, and walls grew lighter with marble lacework. The Renaissance took its time infiltrating the doges' city. I could go on forever leafing through Venice, rendering homage to its great architects, spending time with Andrea Palladio and the white facades of his finest churches, San Giorgio, the Redentore, the Zitelle. There, beauty becomes an order, stone and marble start to obey. There is a balance there, an agreement struck between the rigorous geometry of the shapes. I suddenly believe that architecture is the first of the arts, a state of place that becomes a state of mind. But the obsessive question persists: How is it that, in the end, all these builders understood one another so well? Why, for example, can one say of palazzo Grassi and the Ca' del Duca that they are only fifty meters—not three centuries—apart? How can Baroque architect Longhena and any anonymous Gothic architect be related? Is it because they worked for the same city and the same clients, who had the same requirements and with whom one couldn't be too flexible? Or maybe it is because the light of the lagoon, the emerald glints on the Grand Canal, the gentle air, the tides' slow rhythms, the deep peace of these places made everyone quiet, made them walk and build on tiptoe, from

No other city offers so great a profusion of ornamentation on the facades of its houses, its surrounding walls, the balusters of its staircases, the lintels of its doors, the vaults of its bridges, even the water-level steps of its palaces. There are human heads, and heads of angels, rams, fabulous animals, and monsters, all accentuating the feeling of the baroque that so thoroughly permeates Venice. Life springs from stone, is magnified in stone— while what is human sometimes hides or is transformed behind fixed masks . . . .

one generation to the next. When circumstances— geography and history—force you into cramped promiscuity, the rules of politeness, courtesy, and, of course, urbanity must be pushed to their limits—and what could have been hell becomes heaven instead.

The windows of Professor B.'s vast drawing room look out onto the church of San Pantaleone, between the Frari and campo Santa Margherita (the vault of the church is covered by an immense painting by Fumiani, *The Martyrdom and Glory of Saint Pantaleone*, which always reminds me of some eye-popping Technicolor superproduction). In that drawing room, the professor, one of the most influential people in Venice today, received me.

"Are we burdened by our history?" he asked. "The sociologists have invented the term 'global village' to describe the planet, but Venice, with its neighborhoods and communication networks, has long been the global village." I asked him if he considered himself first a man from a certain neighborhood of Venice, but he ignored my interruption. "We are used to strolling down the alleyways, chatting in shops with very highly skilled artisans. Here, in the parish of San Pantaleone, everyone knows me. I go out into the *campo*, I could never go unnoticed. But fifty or one hundred meters farther away, across a bridge, a *rio*, in another parish, that's not true, and I can lose myself in the city's anonymity."

What did he mean by the burden of history? Of course, Venice is a prisoner of its past; it is also a museum-city. Professor B. began to list all of his city's possible vocations, all the alternative futures he wished it—its European, if not worldwide, cultural vocation; the stimulating center for international meetings that it could be, reviving thereby its oldest tradition. As the drawing room darkened in the early dusk, he spoke with that deliberation, that precise and melancholy courtesy of men of a certain age.

"There are no Italians in Italy," he continued. "No

The intimate beauty of a stone bridge flanked by parapets of Istrian stone (opposite). A sheet drying on a brick wall on the calle dei Preti, a package about to be hauled up with a rope and pulley . . . Everywhere, Venice arranges and reveals still lifes, busy lives, and soul-stirring colors. Porticoes, alleys, cul-de-sacs by canals . . . When you walk in Venice, you enter an extraordinary labyrinth, where you quickly lose your bearings, but gain in return an unlooked-for wisdom: that of always preferring the longer way to the shorter, the beautiful to the practical (following pages).

61

one feels Italian. We have no spirit of nationhood. Here, we feel Venetian. Our culture, our painting, our ways have nothing in common with those of Florence. The fact that we go on foot and live on canals gives us more wisdom. More patience, more serenity? Certainly. Look at Venice's geography. Ask a Venetian for directions. For example: Where is the Accademia? He'll answer by stretching his arm out this way or that—straight out, as you would indicate a nautical course. That's Venice's nautical vocation. Of course, it's impossible to go straight forward in Venice, you have to turn right, left, turn off, take alleyways, bridges, a thousand byways. But you always get there. That's the Venetians' vocation—or genius—for diplomacy!"

"Diplomatic or commercial genius?" I asked. He smiled, with no need to answer, for we both knew that it came to the same thing.

"I almost forgot. Venice is also a feminine city."

"Do you mean a water city?"

"No, I'm not speaking symbolically. I mean that men—the merchants and soldiers—during the Republic were always traveling. They were at sea for months and months. The women stayed home, kept the traditions, held authority in their homes and over their children. Take Goldoni's comedies: the woman

Venice as world capital? Perhaps, after A.D. 1000, when the Serenissima invented capitalism, the income tax, public debt, and financing. Then, all wealth, all news flowed to the city's shores. Today, Venice is more leisurely—

or wiser. They have learned the virtues of far niente. It is enough to follow the world's sound and fury in the newspapers. And reading the Gazzetino is enough for those interested only in local news.

A little girl at the fountain at campo Santa Maria Formosa, a nuns' school near the church of San Aponal. Venice is not just a city for tourists, nostalgists, aesthetes, pensioners, gondoliers, postcard sellers, lovers of the past, and young newlyweds on their honeymoons—it is first and foremost a city that thrills and resounds with the clear laughter of its children.

always has the last word! Venice is the women's city."

I have never met a Venetian who didn't tell me how much he or she loved his or her neighborhood. Is that because the neighborhoods all resemble one another somewhat, with the same *rii*, palazzi, Baroque churches, dilapidated walls, and subtle scent of salt, dust, fish, humidity, faded flowers, and enchantment? Or because all these neighborhoods display the same colors? It is easy to imagine those colors even more iridescent in the eighteenth century, when the palace steps were painted; the frescoes on the outside palace walls were new; and the canal waters reflected the sky, for the tides' supple play cleansed them and people still dredged them. The reason for this universal love of neighborhood lies in the intangible, particular spirit of each of Venice's six *sestieri*—Cannaregio, San Marco, and Castello north of the Grand Canal, and Santa Croce, San Polo, and Dorsoduro south of it (not to mention the island of Giudecca)—of which every inhabitant is proud. One day I heard the Contessa F., in her Grand Canal palace, claim to be able to distinguish the old inhabitants of Cannaregio, Castello, and Dorsoduro by their accents, and it was not too difficult to believe her.

Tired of San Marco and the doges, I sometimes cross the Accademia bridge and go to the Dorsoduro *sestiere*. Life there unfolds more calmly, slowly, wisely. Far from the madding crowds, from the urgency of current events, Venetians suddenly breathe freely. If their city is a theater, I think of Dorsoduro as one of its wings. If their city is a palace, Dorsoduro is the family sitting room. The waters of rio di San Vio and rio Ognissanti are unruffled—no worries. Campo San Trovaso looks like the great deserted square of a small town, whose inhabitants take siestas, write, paint, meditate, do not bother to go out into the streets and face the world's fatigues and disappointments. In fact, Dorsoduro is the *sestiere* of artists, students, painters, writers, all those who want to live

What whimsical spirit prompted the occupant of a small house on the rio della Frescada, across from the Scuola di San Rocco, to adorn the facade with countless little windmills and other painted wood mobiles? It is the same spirit that makes Venice the city of carnival, an ongoing holiday, the city of colors and illusions. The comforting rose-colored reflection of a cloud on a canal in the San Polo neighborhood has the sensual sweetness of a Tiepolo sky.

An impressive view of bridges on the rio di Santa Maria Formosa. Such beauty leaves the cats of Venice indifferent—they belong to no one, but Venice belongs to them. They alone have been able to conquer the city (following pages).

retired from momentary frivolities. Nowhere else could I imagine a Renaissance dwelling on the Grand Canal like the modest palazzo Dario, with its asymmetrical facade, polychrome marbles, stone rosettes on the right, and loggias on three storeys on the left. The slightly Oriental softness of its lines seems to whisper that Venetian culture is more Byzantine than Roman, that it is important to surrender to the intoxication of the senses, and that it is sometimes better to learn to waste one's time than to earn one's living.

The piers of the Zattere run along Dorsoduro's other frontier. I will always see them bathed in late-afternoon sunshine, when the colors are denser. At that hour, the facades of houses, the endless steamers, freighters, and tugs that go down the Giudecca canal, the heavy Corinthian pilasters of the white church of the Gesuiti, the awnings over the terraces of ice-cream parlors no longer seem to absorb light, but rather to give it back, diffuse it with muted impatience, as if to hold back the sunset. It recalls a Belle Epoque decor. Daily life, hardworking and hectic, barely touches the Zattere. Nothing shakes their serenity, not the business of the canal, the Number 5 vaporetti approaching the piers cautiously, nor, across the water, the endless, low, back-lit line of the houses on Giudecca, crushed on the right by the Mulino Stucky's heavy, redbrick masses. Farther out on Giudecca, where the facade of the Redentore twinkles in the dusk that seems to rise from the water, the Zitelle seem—in that "savage" territory—to echo the greatest civilization, and beauty. I suddenly remember a young Venetian woman whom I met through mutual friends one evening at Harry's Bar. Every day she went to work on Giudecca. She described it to us as a terra incognita, a slightly unsettling island peopled with adventurers, prisoners, the working class, and sometimes foul-mouthed street people. "Sometimes I hear them in the cafés. They use expressions, turns of phrase that I don't understand. It's probably just as well

that I don't," she said, with a timid smile that wavered between amusement and fear.

The Castello *sestiere* is another robust and simple world. At the eastern end of Venice lies the forgotten Sant' Elena neighborhood with its wet docks, gardens, playing fields, and the Napoleonic Giardini where the modern-art biennials are held. Technically, Sant' Elena belongs to the Castello district, but its spirit is best summed up in two decors: the Arsenale and the campo Bandiere e Moro, where the church of San Giovanni in Bragora stands.

The Arsenale, a monument to Venetian power since the twelfth century, when the doge Falier nationalized shipbuilding, astonishes visitors. Dante borrowed its most striking settings for his *Inferno*. One can imagine the thousands of specialized workers who labored there during the Renaissance. A galley was assembled in a few hours. It was also where the Venetians invented the assembly line, prefabrication, and express repair shops—but that is another story! Pausing for a moment on the rio del Arsenale to admire the two great sixteenth-century crenelated redbrick towers that flank the water gate of the old Arsenale's wet dock, I can only think of a Hollywood set, a papier-mâché reconstruction of a fortress for a historical epic.

Castello remains certainly the strangest *sestiere* of

Venice. Its residents speak of it wearing the expression of conspirators, as if they didn't want the happiness they feel living there to get around. That happiness seems right at hand—or at heart—on the campo Bandiera e Moro, and then it's gone. The Gothic facade of San Giovanni in Bragora, where Antonio Vivaldi was baptized, rises in its redbrick austerity. Behind its high altar hangs Cima de Conegliano's masterpiece, *The Baptism of Christ*, a painting of absolute simplicity, music, and pure transparency. But I have often found the doors closed, leaving nothing for me to do but wander about the peaceful campo and observe the peaceful old ladies. Seated quietly side by side on benches, they look, in the reassuring immobility of their leisure, united against the flight of time.

Where is the spirit of Cannaregio? Perhaps in the luminous luxury of the campo dei Gesuiti, near the Baroque church of the same name, its facade detailed with angels and saints? Or in the opulent monumentality of the palazzo Labia (today the R.A.I. headquarters building), on the Cannaregio canal, its grand drawing room housing Giambattista Tiepolo's sensuous frescoe, *Anthony and Cleopatra*? No, for the palazzo Labia's luxury and happiness are too dated for one of Venice's liveliest, most modest, and least flashy neighborhoods. Its artisans and shopkeepers are much

The Serenissima's human comedy is played out in the open court-yards of its palaces, with their handsome sculpted wells. This well (below, left) is in the charming, fifteenth-century Casa Goldoni, whose fine staircase leads to the piano nobile. The well in the palazzo Bernardo on the Grand Canal (below, right) is nearly symmetrical. A little covered loggia, or liago, on the facade of the palazzo Minotto, on the banks of the Grand Canal, is surely an opera box for enjoying the show of people, life, and the water (above). The human comedy is at its most vivid in the working-class neighborhoods of Cannaregio (opposite), near the church of San Giobbe, reached by the Tre Archi bridge.

too busy to take much interest in the past. The pretty Gothic cloister of the Madonna dell'Orto is decaying beyond repair. One passes no gondolas full of enraptured tourists: the *rii* San Girolamo and San Alvisi are much too functional and rectilinear to be worth a side trip. Only the heavy barges bearing machine tools or wine flasks use them.

There, in the northern part of Venice, in the center of Cannaregio, the ghetto is contracting. Two ghettoes, to be precise: the *ghetto vecchio*, which dates to 1541, and the *ghetto nuovo*, which, as its name implies, is newer—by twenty-five years. The word "ghetto" almost automatically evokes images of misery, confinement, and persecution. But these were not the case in Venice, where ghettoes and the word for them were devised (from *getar*, the Venetian word for an iron foundry, one of which occupied the island to which the Jews were restricted). Venice is a tolerant city. The Jews were as numerous as they were (around five thousand in the twelfth century) because only the Republic received them—with profitable hospitality. The tall houses that rise in the campo Ghetto Nuovo, gray and austere, look like incredible skyscrapers out of some fantastic medieval tale. But, again, I sense no smell of blood, pogroms, or misery. The tiny *calli* that crisscross the ghetto open onto a vast campo that today belies the proximity of syna-

gogues whose luxury and Baroque elegance ill accord with the Torah's image of a severe God. There I feel I am taking in the essence of Cannaregio, where life is intense, secretive, hardworking; lived day-to-day, modestly, unconcerned with gawkers, idlers, nostalgics, or foreigners. A resident confided to me, "Cannaregio is our last Indian reservation, the last refuge just for Venetians," whether from the entire world or from the other *sestieri*.

I like to take the Mercerie to the Rialto, not because of the jostling tourists or the gaudy shops that all display the same cheap jewelry, the same little glass clowns from Murano, and the same stereotyped carnival masks; but for the transition from the *sestiere* of San Marco to that of San Polo on the other side of the bridge. The San Marco shore is still cosmopolitan. Most of the shops on the Rialto continue the meretricious enticement of tourists. But finally I reach the San Polo side, where like magic the tourists vanish. Beneath the vaults of the covered market, Venetians shop daily. Pyramids of fruit, flowers, vegetables, and farther down, fish, rise in a delicious cacophony of colors. The lemons are a brilliant straw color; the sweet peppers are green and a saffron yellow; the strings of onions are a violet-tinged white. The dark red eggplants reflect the night-blue shadows beneath the arcades.

From San Marco to the *sestiere* San Polo, the smells change as much as the colors. No more leather, ink, eau de Cologne, and sweat. The *erberia*, the produce market, smells of earth, peat, and fresh flowers—these scents mix with those of the modern *pescheria*, the fish market. Here, Venice is no longer made-up or tricked-out—it is once again the city on the lagoon, the great maritime Republic. The heavy odor of gilthead and the acidulated freshness of shrimp attract

A lightning bolt in the sky over the Salute looks like a special effect designed to set off the dramatic beauty of a city where even the doorknobs and doorbells are theatrical props.

prowling cats. Beneath the market's red and green oilcloths, in huge metal tubs, are gray and pink salmon, sardines, trout, and still-shining eels, side by side with the crawling crabs that clamber over one another in a vain attempt to gain freedom. "*Sogliole nostrane*" a sign declares proudly. The octopus, cuttlefish, mussels, and sea perch are also sold as *nostrani*, that is, "local." I can still hear the malicious laugh of a Venetian friend who lives near the Arsenale and who had worked for a time as a fish importer before becoming a journalist.

"There aren't enough in the lagoon or even in the Adriatic," he told me. "The cuttlefish and squid come frozen from Morocco, the sole is almost all from Holland, the burbot comes from France. I remember, in the morning we used to go pick up our crates at the station, where they had come in refrigerated cars. We would transfer our stock to typical Venetian crates, and away we'd go!"

I replied that the rather loose definition of "*nostrano*" didn't bother me. After all, Venice's power and authority had reached very far indeed in centuries past. We were all more or less *nostrani* in Venice.

The *pescheria* cats are in no hurry; they wait their turn. They good-naturedly accept that they are last to be served, like masters of the house. Around one in the afternoon, when the Venetians have finished their marketing, the fish sellers overturn their iron pots, having nothing left to sell; and the *bacari*, the little wine bars, are full throughout the nearby *calli*; then it is the cats' turn to wander around the crates and find their happiness. You always find happiness in Venice.

And the San Polo *sestiere*, which to my mind somewhat resembles that of Santa Croce, may be the happiest one of all.

INTERIORS

Houses, palaces, studios, apartments simple and showy, ancient and modern . . . In Venice, every dwelling is a hidden novel that conveys a long, long history. And every occupant also carries a memory, a passion within. More than any other city in the world, Venice stamps those who have chosen to sleep, love, work, be born, and grow old there. Venetian interiors bear a similar mark, a harmony created by the juxtaposition of centuries of artistic genius. One can—in fact, one must—admire a Venetian interior: the colored beauty of a Murano chandelier, the quality of a terrazzo, the bloom of a stuccowork ceiling, the majesty of a *portego*, the giddy elegance of a Baroque drawing room, the austerity of a gothic relief. One must allow oneself to be overwhelmed by such decor, whether luxurious or modest, and then one may perhaps finally understand why there is a Venetian art of living—a way of living, that is also an art.

Behind La Fenice, in the very heart of Venice, far from the crowds, shops, and glittering *calli*, at the corner of the Verona and San Luca *rii*, is concealed a fifteenth-century palazzo that the guidebooks sometimes call Morà, after its first owner. (What a headache the names of palaces are in Venice! Sometimes they are named for their original occupants, sometimes for their most illustrious owners, sometimes for the currently "reigning" dynasty, sometimes—randomly—for all three at once.) However, the Morà family disappeared long ago. The patrician family that lives here bought it in the middle of the last century, and although the owner who is receiving me can pride himself on descending from one of the most illustrious Venetian lineages, he is, in a sense, a newcomer to the palazzo. For what is a century or two in a city whose history dates back to the Roman Empire?

Here, as in many other Venetian residences, the contrast between the exterior and the interior is strik-

PATRICIAN HOMES

The elegant Gothic Giustinian palace on the Grand Canal encloses a vast courtyard garden (above). One of its most beautiful apartments (opposite) was decorated by the architect Renzo Mongiardino. A fifteenth-century bust of the condottiere Brandolini and a commode decorated with decal designs, a perfect example of so-called arte povera, grace the vestibule area. (Preceding pages) At the Querini-Stampalia museum, a seventeenth-century Carrara marble bust of a bravo *of Francesco Querini's entourage. The* bravi *were much-feared bodyguards in the service of the great patrician families.*

ing. A Gothic palace with ogival windows, it presents a rather austere monumentality along the canals. The decoration of the reception rooms on the *piano nobile*, on the other hand, displays the exquisite elegance of the Venetian eighteenth century, with its double mirrors in the corner of the grand drawing room (one never tires of the multiplication of images and reflections), its furnishings and painted ceilings, its Murano chandeliers. Yet the feeling in these rooms is not so much of parties and dissipation, but of a kind of delicate and happy contemplation. The vestibule walls are decorated with an anonymous and marvelously preserved eighteenth-century fresco on the themes of theater, music, and the worldly comedy. A white parrot faces a young woman who has stuck a rose in her hair. A lute player accompanies the customary gallantries. A cat bristles. Is it due to the warm and muted ocher tones of the frescoes and the room that everything here seems played in a minor key? Levity can be sober, and humor the most serious thing in the world.

I am offered coffee. There is a coffeepot painted in the fresco. The scene is repeated. My host smiles.

"Coffee, of course. In Venice, one begins by drinking coffee, offering coffee—an Oriental tradition. At my father's house, there was always coffee ready on the table. Perhaps we Venetians—with our native indolence and that paralyzing softness that sometimes overtakes us—need this particular stimulant."

Paralyzing softness? On the contrary, the master of the house demonstrates a most tonic energy. We discuss the Venetian genius for diplomacy. Or rather he talks, I listen. He soon turns to the city's present and future.

"I gambled my future on Venice. I gave up everything I had elsewhere to work in Venice, to invest in Venice," he tells me.

And this time I understand better what, in this environment, or in spite of it, appears to be the

Here, the former **portego** was deliberately made smaller in order to make room for a loggia-terrace (above). Simple cane chairs take on an almost princely air overlooking the Grand Canal. A morning room (right) whose discreet elegance appears perfectly natural, as if the decorator's work were invisible.

Mongiardino likes to tell the following anecdote: one day, a Greek student asked Zeno if the latter liked the just-completed Parthenon. After a moment's reflection, Zeno replied, "Yes, because it looks as if it has always been there." As an architect of images, Mongiardino is ruled by this principle. A comfortable living room, its sofas upholstered in rough linen, suffused with light from the canal; a romantic dining room, with its scenic painted wallpapers by Zuber and its trompe l'oeil malachite around doors and moldings; a small television room in warm yellows and reds; an elegant vestibule with perfume-pans on a sideboard; a bedroom—it all seems to have always been there, attaining the ideal elegance.

The doors of this Empire bedroom
are outlined in passementerie
Brandenburgs, the kind of detail
that characterizes Mongiardino's
refined elegance. A painted
plaster dog holds the doors closed

or open. Ventilation of the Venetian palaces is a necessity, not a
luxury, the evenings a cool re-
prieve after the heavy summer
heat.

A pillow on an armchair invites leisure, far niente. The pillow cover is of Venetian lace, of course. In the background, a majestic four-poster bed and a very unusual Empire desk.

opposite of eighteenth-century frivolity. This is no longer simply an historical frame fixed on the memory of fêtes gone by, but a living place whose owner can certainly receive and entertain (his dinners are famous in Venice), but where he mainly lives and works. The past doesn't intimidate him.

The past, however, matters and lingers in the *piano nobile* of the Gothic palazzo Minotto-Barbarigo, across the Grand Canal from the Ca' Dario. The Contessa Maria Franchin, neé Donà dalle Rose, has lived there since 1946. The interior decoration is, again, entirely in the style of the eighteenth century. The vast bedroom is astonishingly beautiful, with wonderfully crafted stuccowork in which scenes from mythology frame the alcove and bed. The ceiling is

(Above) The Pompeian living room on the piano nobile *of the Gothic Minotto Barbarigo palace on the Grand Canal. One of this home's most beautiful rooms is the bedroom, where all the sweet grace of the Venetian eighteenth century is delicately alive. Especially remarkable is the stuccowork around the alcove, the work of two artists from the Ticino, Abbondio Stazio and Carpoforo Mazzetti-Tencalla. On either side of the bed, a Louis XVI gilded wood console supports a ceramic palm tree from Bassano. Is it a vanished era that speaks through this furniture, this stuccowork, these Venetian mirrors and family portraits (following pages), as if the past were preserved under dustcovers?*

by a student of Tiepolo. A fragile dressing table stands patiently in a corner of the room.

Walking from room to room through this palace is like making a pilgrimage to bygone days. There is a delicate pastel signed by Rosalba Carriera, a Pompeian-style sitting room, some stunning stuccowork enclosing brightly colored animals in medallions: rabbit, duck, hedgehog, owl, tortoise. But the countess is most justly proud of her little covered panoramic balcony, built in the last century and called, in Venice, a *liago*. Few Venetian palaces are so privileged. She enjoys making herself comfortable there and observing the teeming life of the Grand Canal, the passing gondolas and vaporetti, the to and fro of the Santa Maria del Giglio *traghetto*. Then she goes back into her palace, leaving behind the world's

Like many other Gothic homes, the apartments of palazzo Mora, not far from La Fenice, were entirely redone in the eighteenth century. This is evident in the main living room (above, left) with its Tiepolesque painted ceiling and flooring of typical terrazzo alla veneziana. In a hallway (above, right), a bust of an ancestor of the patrician family that has lived in the palazzo for one hundred and fifty years.

A servant bringing coffee, a cat . . . the living room's eighteenth-century frescoes narrate in eloquent detail the daily life of the Venetian nobles.

These charming frescoes seem to portray the life of the Venetian nobles as infused with a festive, flirtatious, and theatrical spirit—no anachronism, in fact, for on summer evenings, the owner enjoys hosting dinners on the palace's large terrace. A trompe-l'oeil parrot on a balustrade recalls the Venetian love of pets. A nineteenth-century banquette (left), curiously, displays the same decorative motifs.

spectacle for the past's twilight beauty.

What nuance of light or intangible balance of shapes evokes, in a room, a feeling of euphoria or melancholy, paralysis or dynamism? This bright, expansively elegant apartment on the top floor of the Gothic Pisani-Moretta palace, the home of Girolama Sammartini, overlooks the Grand Canal from a vast terrace. The blinding white Istrian stone accentuates the azure of the sky and the monochrome marbles and pargeting across the Grand Canal. One can just see the cupolas of Saint Mark's above the rooftops. This is, to me, the most beautiful view of Venice, because of the impression of pure luminosity and expansiveness that one so rarely feels when plunged in the heart of the city, in the network of its alleyways and canals.

One of Girolama's brothers, Maurizio Sammartini, has been restoring the palace's *piano nobile* for years, and rents out its great Baroque salons, with ceilings painted by Tiepolo and Angeli, for receptions. Centuries ago, Venetians were notorious for sacrificing everything for show, and one entered their homes only by the canal entrance—nothing on the other sides referred to that single outward splendor. Today, to reach the palazzo Pisani-Moretta on foot, one has to take a dark and forbidding *calle*. Inside reigns the spirit of the eighteenth century, with pretty, delicately tinted stuccowork, Carpioni paintings framed

The delightful paintings on the cupboards of the large boudoir-storeroom in this top-floor apartment of the palazzo Pisani-Moretta (right), are by the eighteenth-century Venetian artist Diziani. A pair of old Este vases in the dining room (below). Even in the attic of this palace, with its original sumptuous Gothic facade, the rooms are vast and almost euphorically elegant. There is a reason: during the cold months, the wealthy owners would leave the lower floors for these low-ceilinged—and thus more easily heated—apartments.

The originally Gothic palazzo Corner-Gheltoff-Alverà underwent alterations in the sixteenth and seventeenth centuries. The wood and glass partition that divides its portego (above, left) was put in by the Count Paolo Alverà early in this century. The portego, a great hall that usually crosses the older Venetian palaces, in the Middle Ages served as showroom and salesroom for the goods of the merchant-patricians. The glass set into lead, or vetro piombato, is a recurring decorative motif in Venetian art. In the portego, a Murano chandelier (above, right) illuminates the piano at which the owner's eldest daughter enjoys practicing.

On the dining-room walls hang a unique set of etchings after Canaletto's twelve feast-days of Venice. A parquet floor from the presbytery of Saint Mark's takes the place of the traditional terrazzo. The table is set with a

white damask cloth, eighteenth-century Murano glasses, a little silver and enamel salt cellar, and hand-painted china plates by Richard Ginori. There is a handsome collection of copper pots and pans in the kitchen.

in the wood paneling of the sitting room, and old Este vases in the dining room. Here, however, there is no stifling deference to the sumptuous decor; this is simply a home.

The same energy prevails in the home of the Conte Paolo Alverà and his wife, Ketty, in the palazzo Corner-Gheltoff, which was originally Gothic but partially altered in the sixteenth and seventeenth centuries. The Alverà family has owned this palace on the Grand Canal near San Samuele for two hundred years. Having recently returned to Venice, Paolo's move into the *piano nobile* was prompted by a love for the past and a greater belief in living in the present. The moral is clear: It is not enough to live in the beauty of once-upon-a-time; one must also not give it too much attention, and move through it naturally. This is a home where one lives under the aegis of original eighteenth-century Venetian etchings lit by Murano chandeliers. The traditional terrazzo was replaced at the turn of this century by a parquet floor from the Saint Mark's presbytery. In this place, civilization is not for museums but for people. Here, Venice palpitates, unembalmed.

With charming modesty, the Contessa L. speaks of her sixty-square-yard, canal-level home in the Gothic palazzo Bernardo as her "gondolier's apartment." In fact, the Venetian palaces were once veritable residential complexes, in which different branches of the same family lived on different floors. The palazzi also served as warehouses and showrooms, and artisans rented rooms on the ground floors, as did gondoliers. Today, by her window overlooking the Grand Canal, the Contessa L. works in petit point, makes splendid bouquets of multicolored beads, and listens to Tartini violin concerti. She loves Venice for the ever-changing colors of the water, whose reflected light tints her apartment. Nineteenth-century French

The Countess L. lives in a small apartment on the ground floor of the elegant Gothic Bernardo palace. She modestly calls it her "gondolier's apartment"—at times, she must barricade the bottom of the door with boards as a defense against the redoubtable acqua alta (opposite, top). Making the most of every little nook, she was able to transform a tiny space into a precious retreat. A large, Romantic-era French painted wallhanging in the sitting room (opposite, bottom right). The Countess L. enjoys embroidering gifts for friends by the window—bouquets whose flowers are made up of colored beads—or else, as here, making lovely lace-lined workboxes (above).

painted wallpaper makes the place seem larger, and a whispered happiness reigns here, where several gondoliers' chairs are arranged.

It is difficult, on the other hand, to describe the very special atmosphere of the rooms of the Conte and Contessa A., on the *piano nobile* of their palace (the former palazzo Giustinian), built in the mid-fifteenth century and not far from the Ca' Foscari. There is an obvious theatricality, but it gives way to an unexpected intimacy. Everything here hits the right note—almost too right. Disarray of styles becomes a nice artistic touch. The beauty of a particular piece of furniture matters less than the mood of the room it is in. In any case, there is no sense of Wagner present, even though he composed part of the second act of *Tristan und Isolde* here. In this room, we are more in the spirit of Italian opera, and its set designer, so to speak, is Renzo Mongiardino, who designed opera sets before becoming one of the most famous interior architects of our time. His were the sets for Maria Callas's *Tosca* at Covent Garden and for Zeffirelli's *Un Ballo in maschera* at La Scala.

At the A. home, Romantic-era etchings glow beneath eighteenth-century chandeliers. A canopy bed is unoffended by comfortable modern armchairs. Chinese vases and nineteenth-century consoles fit agreeably into a Neoclassical environment. The loggia over the Grand Canal is a winter garden, with rustic cane armchairs. Is that a rich marquetry desk framed by a doorway? Not at all, it is only a rare and perfect example of *arte povera*, a simple piece of wood furniture on which etchings were glued and varnished to give the illusion of lavish marquetry. The goal of all illusion is to merge with the natural, and one would never guess this was produced. Mongiardino can congratulate himself—he has succeeded because he has disappeared. In such a place, one is moved to live, not to admire.

Tell me where you live, how you live, and I will tell you who you are. This adage is most true in Venice. The city marks its inhabitants, sometimes forging them exceptional destinies that their homes embody. The beauty and harmony of these homes are never conventional or repetitious. They are all Venetian and all unique because they are inhabited by personalities.

Some of the most outstanding individuals I have had the opportunity to meet have this in common: they don't just live in Venice, they devote most of their lives to it. The Baronessa Maria Teresa Rubin de Cervin, who lives in the palazzo Albrizzi, has been director of the Venice office of UNESCO since 1975, fighting to preserve and restore the city's architectural beauty. The Contessa Ileana Chiappini di Sorio, who lives in the palazzetto Contarini, teaches art history at the University of Venice, preserving the city's cultural memory. Professor B., in his tranquil home on campo San Pantaleone, has reached retirement age but is still a procurator of Saint Mark's, administering the city's greatest shrines. Natale Rusconi, who calls the Zattere home, manages the Hotel Cipriani, endowing Venice with the most opulent hospitality. Bruno Tosi, who resides in the palazzo Malipiero Trevisan in Santa Maria Formosa, describes himself as journalist, writer, producer of the Carnival, and founder of *Omaggio a Venezia*, setting the Serenissima to celebration and music. And the Contessa M., who lives in vast house on Giudecca, has, since the death of Mariano Fortuny in 1949, run the workshops of the same name. Here the finest fabrics are printed, perpetuating the Serenissima's legendary elegance and material.

Tell me where you live . . . the palazzo Albrizzi, built at the end of the sixteenth century and added onto two hundred years later, displays a curious characteristic: it is both the most imposing and the most

VENETIAN PROFILES

Concealed behind campo San Polo, the monumental seventeenth-century palazzo Albrizzi (above) has retained its magnificent period interior and brilliantly imaginative stuccowork. Maria Teresa Rubin de Cervin, director of the Venice office of UNESCO, lives on the third and top floor. What surprises is the size of the large living room (opposite), with its eighteenth-century pieces and rather low ceiling decorated with baroque stuccowork. The flooring is the traditional terrazzo alla veneziana. A hall lined with bookshelves and lit by two bull's-eye windows runs the length of the living room (following pages). Up against this partition, a satin-covered Louis XVI banquette and armchairs.

secret palace in the city. Maria Teresa Rubin de Cervin lives on the third and top floor. The contrast is striking between the vastness of the rooms and the low ceilings, resulting in a twofold effect—a precious feeling of size and intimacy. One can see Venice through the windows, its campanili and the red-tiled roofs. A library-hallway runs the length of the drawing room like a gallery. Bull's-eyes let in light and views. As in many other Venetian palaces, the flooring is the famous terrazzo, a sort of putty matrix holding bits of colored marble.

"I lead a very unworldly life," says Maria Teresa Rubin de Cervin. "The receptions are intended principally for people passing through, foreigners. The French enjoy Carnival more than the Venetians do, and I confess that I care more about the Venetians. The most important churches and palaces have often been saved from ruin, but what about the lesser and often more dilapidated sites? The people who live there can't afford to restore them, so Milanese or Americans buy them. After saving Venice, will we have to save the Venetians?"

A century or two ago, women in society had certain indispensable accessories used when flirting, chief among them, the fan. A collector of fans, the Countess Chiappini di Sorio occupies a relatively modest palace tucked away not far from Santa Maria Formosa. The court, typical of the second half of the sixteenth century, has an elegant well—renovated, like the rest of the building, in the eighteenth century—and retains a quality that is both severe and pleasing. The shadows are deep beneath its portico and in the muted red of its brick walls. But in the reception rooms everything is reserved, bright, and musical. In one room after another, the mistress of the house has arranged a harmonium, a Venetian piano, a Pianola, a zither, a small violin, and a balalaika. And on the walls, the fans are pinned under glass.

An entomologist of Venice's bygone days and a historian, the Contessa Chiappini di Sorio points out her best pieces—eighteenth- and nineteenth-century Venetian, French, English, and Chinese fans of Bruges lace and painted paper. All display the same fragile and tinted and ephemerally beautiful elegance.

I say that the fan—which flatters the gaze and masks the woman, at once mirage and screen, desire and frustration—is in keeping with a typically Venetian art of living, a form of long-ago intrigue.

"You're right," she replies. "But a fan is also a way of holding a conversation, the silent conversation between a lady and her *cavalier servente*, with its extremely strict codes, a language of pure seduction."

At the other extreme, is it to evoke the Serenissima's warlike, conquering tradition that Professor B. has in his home a collection of military helmets from around the world? (He had been missing that of the Paris Republican Guard until the president of the French Republic, François Mitterand, recently gave him one.) And is it to recall the opulent Venetian observance of the Catholic religion that he keeps an astonishing array of antique chasubles embroidered in gold and silver? Actually, I don't think so. Collectors mainly just follow their fancies, what they chance upon, the wandering notions that strike them. And in Professor B.'s vast apartment on the *piano nobile* of a Gothic

The Countess Ileana Chiappini di Sorio, professor of art history at the University of Venice, has endowed her apartments in the former Contarini palace with a charming, cheerful elegance, embodied by her Venetian baroque furniture and, on the walls, a collection of eighteenth- and nineteenth-century fans from Venice, France, England, and China, of Bruges lace. On a graceful piano, made in Venice in 1800, an album of old daguerreotypes (below). The courtyard of the palace (above) is typical of the second half of the sixteenth century, although the well was renovated in the eighteenth century, as was the rest of the building.

palace on campo San Pantaleone, in the paintings by Maffei and other seventeenth-century Baroque painters, in the books piled on his desk and filling his library, in the fine set of Murano glasses, I perceive the double, complementary sign of elegance and pure fantasy, the apparent disorder of a real place of work and reflection, and the demanding search for a sometimes self-consciously bizarre beauty. To put it another way, at Professor B.'s there reigns a very rare feeling of freedom—that of the life that has accumulated there, mixed with the caprices of an alert intelligence.

Is Bruno Tosi's apartment on the *piano nobile* of palazzo Malpiero—with its Florentine-style dining room dominated by a Della Robbia fountain and its D'Annunzian bedroom—a livable apartment? It seems, theatrical above all, a stage set to receive guests.

The opposite is true of the charming retreat on the Zattere that is home to Natale Rusconi and Connie, his American-born wife. "Retreat" is the only word . . . I like to imagine its owner across the canal at the Hotel Cipriani, on Giudecca, when he is done welcoming his distinguished guests and overseeing the thousand details of the gigantic enterprise. I imagine him anxious to relax in what could indeed be a

Venice is a city defined by music, and music is everywhere in the home of the Countess Chiappini di Sorio. Beneath a Murano chandelier, this morning room is host to a fin-de-siècle Viennese piano and, against the wall and between Louis XVI chairs, a harmonium.

Professor B., formerly professor of constitutional law, presently procurator of Saint Mark's Basilica, is unquestionably one of the most prominent people in Venice. He lives on the piano nobile of a Gothic palace in campo San Pantaleone. He is a dedicated collector, and particularly proud of his Turkish, Venetian, Spanish, and German chasubles from the fifteenth to seventeenth centuries, and of his unusual set of military helmets.

Producer of the Venice carnival, journalist, and writer Bruno Tosi lives on the piano nobile of a palace in campo Santa Maria Formosa. His apartment is more Florentine in inspiration than Venetian, even if the dining room table is lit by two Murano chandeliers. A Renaissance mantelpiece adds a severe note to a room the jewel of which is undoubtedly the great terra-cotta fountain. As a centerpiece, eighteenth-century Bassano cherubs (right).

104

This living room of a Gothic palace near the Ca' Dario is suffused with a delicate, milky light that seems to rise from the Grand Canal. The gilded-wood framed mirror, the painted wood chairs, and the trestle table evoke eighteenth-century Venice. A Second Empire circular couch, or *borne*, adds a precious note of comfort.

The director of the Hotel Cipriani, Natale Rusconi, lives in a charming house on the Zattere. In the small front garden, a stone bench invites one to rest in the cool twilight. The house was originally two small, fifteenth-century fisherfolks' houses joined together in the last century. A unique feeling of comfort, of well-being, reigns in the house.

On the wall (above, right), a nineteenth-century Neapolitan Impressionist painting, and, framed by the bookcase, a sofa covered in fabric by Rubelli. The armchairs are upholstered in petit point.

The everyday dining room, adjoining the kitchen, is certainly one of the warmest, most intimate rooms in the house. Two Sicilian taper stands are set before the fireplace.... And always this wonderful garden opening onto the lagoon, its old well spouting green plants.

refuge. One pushes open a little door on the embankment (not far from the modest and charming Pensione Seguso) and crosses an unexpected garden overrun with ferns, ramblers, and Virginia creeper to get to the house—originally two fisherfolks' houses on three storeys that were opened into each other. It seems as if no accident or misfortune could ever happen in a house so instilled with a warm and cheering domestic intimacy of which Anglo-Saxons sometimes hold the secret. Elegance merges with comfort. The formal dining room is Chippendale, decorated with fine nineteenth-century faiences from Nove (near Bassano), and the moiré drapes in the beautiful drawing room are by Rubelli. Yet one might prefer the delightful kitchen—dining room, where Natale and Connie keep their collection of cookbooks from all over the world (and practice their gastronomic discoveries).

One is always sorry to leave this house. Countrified, refined refuges are so rare in Venice! Their gardens obviously have nothing in common with the Countess M.'s on Giudecca, where statues of Istrian stone converse from the corners of flower beds. The shade beneath the trees is cool, and the foliage hides the monumental and lugubrious silhouette of the Mulino Stucky. A pool adds an odd note of Roman nobility to this place adjoining the famous Fortuny

On Giudecca, behind the Fortuny workshops, a private park spreads over five acres. Within it rises a house watched over by this seventeenth-century English statue in its niche. Mariano Fortuny, the brilliant inventor, the man who dressed the beauties of the Belle Époque and Marcel Proust's heroines, kept his printing and dyeing processes secret. The gardens of Giudecca are often secret, too, sheltered behind houses and high walls. This garden counts many fruit trees, and boasts a swimming pool and a 1950s-style living room veranda (opposite).

workshops. Only a few initiates know the secrets of dyeing and printing that produce, on long-fibered Egyptian cottons specially made for Fortuny, or on other, more precious fabrics, the effects of light and color—willow-green, beige, brilliant red, and gold —in short, all those marvelous motifs composed by Mariano Fortuny y Madrazo until his death in 1949.

"No, of course there are no secrets, tricks, or magic formulas," explained a young woman who works here. "Everything is empirical, artisanal. Look at this fabric! There is an irregularity in the printing. It depends on the day, the temperature, the humidity, the season. If something is wrong, we have to work back up the dyeing process, using trial and error to find the fault, and pick up the intuitions Fortuny had sixty years ago."

A legendary figure, Fortuny was born in Grenada in 1871. He clothed Isadora Duncan and the elegant ladies of the Belle Epoque, as well as Marcel Proust's heroines. Fortuny—painter, sculptor, inventor, brilliant decorator. . . . Perhaps he is still there, in those Giudecca gardens, if not in the Contessa M.'s home, so perfectly decorated one would never guess it was a modern house. Perhaps the Serenissima can confer an instant patina on all that is built in its territory, endow with Venetian light an Empire dining room, English silverware, and a flight of steps in a stairwell.

It seems impossible that the home of the present owner of the firm of Fortuny was built thirty years ago. The wrought-iron staircase, with its splendid eye-shaped run, is her own design. The doors onto the landing are rosewood marquetry. A Venetian mirror, a Louis XVI console and chairs (right). Everything is in keeping: the embroidered cushions, the tapestry on the armchairs (below, a model of the pozzotto armchair), carpet, and hangings. The morning room is decorated with eighteenth-century architectural plans of Palladian villas (above).

In an Empire dining room, Louis XVI candelabra. The floor is of Carrara marble. The wall is covered in "Lucrezia," a Fortuny fabric. On the walls hang Carpioni paintings on the theme of the four seasons.

The morning room (right) is furnished with comfortable armchairs and sofas covered in another Fortuny fabric, "Olympia." On either side, pieces of Davenport china.

112

On the dining room table, a handsome service of English silverware and chandeliers wrapped in tissue paper. The precaution is necessary because the air of Venice is sometimes so humid that it carries germs or tiny algae that proliferate on every surface. (Left) A Romantic-era piece of English china.

It is not surprising that Venetian interiors are sometimes festive, if not spectacular. After all, Carnival lasted six months in the eighteenth century, like the endless Indian summer of the Republic's decline. The Serenissima no longer dreamed of conquering new territories, negotiating rich new treaties, or fighting with new fleets, but only of perfecting the difficult art of living happily. The play of masks, pleasures, encounters, music, banter, chance, and love took place not only along the canals, on gondolas in the shelter of the *felze*, in the *campielli*, the *ridotti*, and the ballrooms, but filtered through the entire city, bringing its wit, sensual grace, and taste for make-believe into its very interiors.

At the turn of the century, Henri de Regnier could still refer, with almost incredulous fascination, to the costume balls given by the Marquise V. at the old palazzo Venier, complete with a gold-painted nude pianist and young leopards on display—prudently injected with morphine, however, before they were introduced into society. The days are well and truly gone of the great, mad, "decadent" parties where Venice burned itself out, ruined itself with unparalleled elegance. And yet, today the February Carnival revives a bit of that climate of elegant dissipation. On the piazza San Marco one passes powdered gentlemen, young ladies in dominoes, seducers in black *bauta* and white *maschera*, and Oriental princesses escorted by unlikely Marco Polos. There is in Venice one man who still keeps up the spirit of the Serenissima, its receptions, its disguises, its masks, its gaiety. His name: the Count Emile Targhetta d'Audiffret. About a dozen years ago, he moved to Venice and the palazzo Merati on the Fondamenta Nuove, on the corner of rio dei Mendicanti, across from the lagoon and San Michele Island. Although he is a newcomer to modern Venice, however, his spirit is that of Casanova's, Vivaldi's, or Goldoni's Venice.

His friends say, with more affection than irony:

VENETIAN EXTRAVAGANCE

As his Venetian friends well know, the Count Emile Targhetta d'Audiffret more often sports carnival costumes than three-piece suits; he wants to perpetuate the Serenissima's spirit of endless holiday. By a curious coincidence, he lives on the piano nobile of the lovely seventeenth-century palazzo Merati, at the corner of rio dei Mendicanti and the Fondamenta Nuove—where none other than Giacomo Casanova's mother and two sisters lived.

"There are two sights that foreigners must not miss in Venice: the Doges' Palace and the Count Targhetta." He is a man who has turned his life into a never-ending party, who makes Carnival last six months, eight months, all year long. For him, disguise is not a pastime, but a way of life. He changes centuries as if changing handkerchiefs (or costumes). "It is not enough to wear a costume, you must also be at ease in your costume, embody it, in a sense. That is the true secret of Carnival," he tells me. He devotes himself with a loving and learned meticulousness to designing new outfits, which he makes himself, out of fabric, plastic, and *strass*. In his view, luxury is always only the appearance of luxury. The false becomes the material of choice for real disguises. And nothing is more fun than what is fake.

During the 1990 Carnival, the Venice daily paper, *Il Gazzettino*, described the Count Targhetta as a man *"ormai inesorabilmente convinto di vivere davvero nel diciasettesimo secolo"* ("by now inexorably convinced that he is really living in the seventeenth century"). The statement seems dubious to me, especially in its use of the word *"davvero."* No, the Count Targhetta is well aware that there is nothing "real" about Venice—or else that true and false exchange attributes, centuries exchange privileges, and people exchange their identities. He knows very well who he is: a man of the present, the past, and of an immortal Venice that prefers the shadow to the substance.

Casanova's mother and sisters lived in the Merati palace. They say that the legendary seducer took refuge there when he tried—in vain—to elude the Republic's *sbirri*, who locked him into the notorious Piombi. Living, in a way, under the tutelary presence of Giacomo Casanova, who raised seduction to a fine art, can only delight the Count Targhetta, whose faithful servant, Michele, sometimes sports costumes as extravagant as his master's. The whirling stuccowork of the bedroom alcove and of the *portego's* double

The Count Targhetta, a designer of sumptuous fancy dress, loves illusion in all its forms—he adjusts and embellishes the past. He enjoys painting fake Longhis and Canalettos. The ceiling beams in his portego are decorated with paper bands painted to look like malachite. But the fine painting resting on an easel in the back of the portego is not a fake. It is the Portrait of the Maréchal de Schulemburg, by Hansius—once Louis XV's official painter. The stuccowork around the double front doors (right), signed by Abbondio Stazio and Carpoforo Mazzetti-Tencalla, is virtually unequalled in Venice for its richness and virtuosity.

Venice and the home of the Count Targhetta are stages, and the count's servant, Michele, is as ready to don disguises on occasion as his employer. His every appearance is an entrance.

More magnificent stuccowork by Stazio and Mazzetti-Tencalla decorates the count's bedroom alcove. In the portego, a fine Louis XV wall-clock above two Dresden china dogs—a breed that was once all the rage in Venice.

The Milanese director Pier Luigi Pizzi lives in an apartment on the piano nobile of the early-sixteenth-century palazzo Contarini dalle Figure on the Grand Canal. Pizzi chose the architect Foscari to do the interior design.

The theatrical dining room, with its late-sixteenth-century fireplace and frieze of paintings bordering the early-seventeeth-century ceiling, appears to await, with its several tables, a large company.

The styles and moods of various centuries collide here: modern couches and armchairs in the drawing room (above), as well as in the adjacent sitting room (left), busts in the ancient fashion, Renaissance fireplace (opposite, bottom). But the obelisks give the whole a spare feeling and a very Neoclassic kind of elegance. No surprise to those who saw, for example, Pizzi's production of Berlioz's Troyens, which inaugurated the Opera de la Bastille in Paris. The obelisks, sphere, and busts are actually of painted wood, props designed by Pizzi and created by his crew.

doors are signed by Abbondio Stazio and Carpoforo Mazzetti-Tencalla, and offer testimony to the imagination and absolute intoxication of the senses of which the age of enlightenment held the dark secret, so to speak. On the wall of the *portego*, a valuable Louis XV wall clock has long since stopped telling time. To what end would it do so? Here, the time difference is measured in centuries, not in hours.

Pier Luigi Pizzi, the decorator, scenographer, and opera set designer, is either the most Venetian of Milanese or the most Parisian of Venetians—when he is not relaxing in another of his Italian homes, living the simple life in Castel Gandolfo, for example, near the pope's residence. He follows his whims, his moods, and his work, too, depending upon whether La Scala, the Paris Opéra, or La Fenice asks him to cast his spell over Handel, Rameau, or Rossini. With his sharp laughter, penetrating gaze, and short, salt-and-pepper beard, Pizzi is the perfect Renaissance or Baroque gentleman. He dwells on the *piano nobile of*

Actress Valentina Cortese's apartment, in a house on Giudecca, is astonishing in its swirling euphoria. The paintings under glass in her bedroom are inspired by the decor of the Café Florian. A pair of dancing slippers rests on an armchair, whose silver-plated frame recalls the style of Indian maharajas. The living room of the actress—who appeared with Ava Gardner in The Barefoot Contessa—*refers back to the age of music and operetta, with a fresco by a student of Mongiardino, ebonized pearwood furniture with mother-of-pearl inlays, flowers, and delicate colors.*

120

A plate and glasses from Murano; a handsome carnival tricorn with a lace veil to conceal the face; Second Empire parrot sconces; Louis XVI enamel place settings by Puiforcat; amusing ceramic statuettes from Bassano; other, etched, glasses from Murano ... Valentina Cortese isn't afraid of clutter. Hers is the apartment of a collector, a lover of rare objects who can integrate her sense of beauty with personal flights of fancy. Everything reveals a certain talent for living. In Paris, she enjoys rummaging through antique stores and flea markets, bringing her booty back to Venice.

the palazzo Contarini, a Lombard Renaissance palace on the Grand Canal. The palazzo is known as *"delle figure"* because of the two great statues, like caryatides, that flank the entrance porch and appear to be supporting the facade's central balcony. There is nothing "realistic" or down-to-earth, no mundane comfort in his apartment, "revised" by the architect Foscari. The dining room doesn't just have a table, it has two, three, six, more than one can count. Like an opera chorus, the guests will be arriving soon, the candelabra will be lit. Obelisks set the rhythm of the other rooms—but is this stage set Baroque, Neoclassical, or Postmodern? In Pizzi's home, life is a show. The art of living is the art of staging one's life.

Is Valentina Cortese's enchanting apartment in Guidecca, not far from Casa Frollo, the set for an opera or an operetta? One enters it as into a luscious Second Empire fondant. There is no question that an actress lives here, and though she costarred with Ava Gardner in *The Barefoot Contessa*, it is a pleasure to imagine her in the most alluring little shoes. Everything here has a story—a love story—cushions, paintings, jewelry, flowers, statuettes, embroidered tablecloths, champagne flutes. This piece of furniture is from an antiques shop on Paris's Quai Voltaire. That knick-knack is from the Puces. And what can one say about her bedroom, with its paintings under glass recalling those at the Café Florian? Are we still on stage?

In François Truffaut's *La Nuit américaine*, Valentina Cortese parodied with irresistible humor and brio the character of an extravagant diva. Don't misunderstand me—I see neither parody nor extravagance in her Venetian apartment. On the contrary, I am touched by its total sincerity, the sincerity of an existence that wishes to be festive, to see life through rose-colored glasses rather than in a brown study, in music rather than words, where there are never enough flowers in the vases, arabesques in movement, and sparkle in

This home, its walls attractively pargeted, runs along the rio della Salute. The little garden (opposite), the terraces, the balcony, and the windows open onto one of the most beautiful views of Venice, from Giudecca to the palaces of the Grand Canal.

crystal. It is perhaps a kind of philosophy.

I recall the "ideal" house in Dorsoduro, behind the Salute, with its balconies, terraces, and gardens overlooking one of the most beautiful perspectives in the world—the volutes of a Baroque church, glimpses of Giudecca and the Grand Canal, splendid sunsets. Here, the show is outdoors, with the house accommodating the audience. Or perhaps the show is indoors, where luxury and shimmering decors are backdrops for a never-ending show on the art of living.

The slender, distinguished, and voluble owner of this home never takes for granted the privilege of living at the heart of a mirage. And though Venice-born, she says so in the simplest, most unaffected way:

"Venice, Venice *meravigliosa*"—she uses this word constantly, ringing all the tonic changes possible on it—"I'm dreaming, this is impossible, I tell myself I will wake up one day. Look at those colors out here, the canals! How can one be bored for even a moment in Venice? Beauty is everywhere, inexhaustible. . . ."

There is beauty in her home, too, in the paintings by Carpioni, Sebastiano Ricci, and Maffei; in the dining room's paneling and mirrors from a Roman palace, beneath a most theatrically draped ceiling; in a delicate painted-wood harpsichord across which ivory elephants from Ceylon march; in the image of silver ships on a console, setting sail for unknown shores; in the twelve small seventeenth-century paintings that portray the months of the year and share the drawing room with an imposing Austrian ceramic stove.

However, the point is not to make an inventory, but, on the contrary, to let oneself explore the tender confusion of a beauty as diffuse as an enchantment. Common sense often uses the phrase "too beautiful to be true," and common sense is not always mistaken. In that phrase, Venice is not "true." This Venetian home is infused with festivity—and perfect illusion.

Ceylonese ivory elephants caparisoned with precious stones march across a small painted harpsichord at the back of the dining room. On a console, an eighteenth-century miniature model in silver of a sixteenth-century Spanish ship. In the dining room, a highly theatrical tented ceiling, wood paneling, and mirrors from a Roman palace.

An Austrian ceramic stove holds
pride of place in the morning
room. On the walls, a series of
eighteenth-century Venetian
paintings signed by Maggiotto,
one of Piazzetta's pupils, depicts
allegories of the twelve months.
On a sideboard, a collection of
checkered silver boxes.

There are very few public gardens in Venice. The geometric Napoleonic Gardens must be mentioned for the record. They are exiled near Sant' Elena and, by definition, have nothing to do with the history of the Republic. On the other hand, Venice conceals far more precious gardens— secret gardens. Why are they secret? Because the Venetians pamper them like tender confidants, and because they are priceless, and like priceless things are better enjoyed discreetly, not displayed as an obnoxious manifestation of wealth. One keeps one's jewels in jewelry boxes, and stores them in strong-boxes. Venice's gardens are tucked away behind high walls, sheltered from the gaze and envy of strangers, of the spiteful, of passers-by, and of barbarians.

Generally speaking, Venice lacks two very simple things: land and sky. The first Venetians had to fight foot by foot, so to speak, to build their city, conquer the lagoon, and make the most of every surface to consolidate their ground, drive their pilings, and raise their shanties and their palaces. Land and space are their ultimate luxuries. That is why one winds one's way along impossibly narrow *calli*, why palazzi, churches, and modest homes are constantly jostling for room, why there are so few open spaces in this city. Pedestrians in Venice rarely see the sky; it is up there somewhere, a narrow ribbon between two cornices. One must climb up to meet it, and there Venice finally breathes freely, reconnecting the expansive tenderness of sea air, clouds, and the lagoon.

Venice's gardens climb, too. They have no other way to spread out or compete with either nature's great expanses or the great symmetries of the Renaissance spirit. Forbidden all horizontality, they climb boldly skyward. Venice's cypresses look like campanili. Virginia creeper and ivy scale the palaces. The ramblers *must* climb. Grapevines wrap around their trellises; wisteria clings to facades. To find Venice's gardens, strollers must raise their heads and inhale the

GARDENS

The owners of Venice's gardens maintain them, hide them, cherish them passionately. They are especially precious because every inch of land has been wrested from the water of the lagoon. They therefore take advantage of the tiniest space, even climbing along walls. (Opposite) A detail of the garden adjoining the Fortuny workshops on Giudecca.

perfumes of honeysuckle and jasmine, must seek out leaves and the obstinate rank weeds that thrust their roots into crevices of stone and brick. This is how one discovers the Ca' Dario's little garden from a pretty bridge in Dorsoduro, past the Guggenheim Foundation. Rather, one imagines it, like some inaccessible Eden, whose massy rhododendrons, azaleas, and oleanders one detects by smell on the other side of its walls.

And what do the Venetians do? They climb even faster than their gardens do, reaching (the example of the Ca' Dario is again relevant) their *altane*, the wooden terraces, or squat belvederes they have built on the roofs of their homes. There they have sky, sun, and light. Venetian women dry their hair there, giving it the warm, soft glow of the famous Titian red. And there the men relax, far from the city and its cares. The Serenissima is a city one leaves vertically.

The Venetians have always kept very accurate count of their riches. So they could say, in 1603, that the San Marco area had exactly thirty-nine gardens, Dorsoduro, twenty-nine, and Cannaregio, forty. Among the latter, I wish to mention the one around the Casinò degli Spiriti (*"spiriti"* in the sense of noted wits, of course, not ghosts). It bordered the lagoon and was where Aretino, Titian, and Sansovino met for leisurely discourse. It still exists, though in a distressingly neglected state, but it is accessible only to the pensioners at the convent-hospital that owns it. In any history of the Serenissima, the fortunes of its gardens would prove instructive indeed. For example, one might contrast its earliest, exuberant green spaces with the Renaissance gardens, which evidence the new passions of the age for the sciences and botany. The seventeenth century would witness the invasion of lemon tress, which were then new to the region, while the eighteenth century manifested the lucidity and order of the French influence, for example, in the Ca' Zenobio gardens. And then there are the vigorous statements of a painter like Hundert-

(Right) In the peaceful Dor-soduro neighborhood, at the end of campo San Vio, rises a former chapel, today the home of the decorator Pietro Pinto. A garden envelops it in silence—even the lions are still.

In these vast Giudecca gardens (above), seventeenth-century statues, Adonis and Venus, flirt between two clusters of trees. An ancient stone well (right) adorns the center with a plant motif.

Whether on Giudecca (above) or in the little garden of the rio Marin palace that inspired the interiors of Henry James's Aspern Papers, the gardens of Venice are the result of human efforts more than nature's. The Venetians consider them architecture, outdoor drawing rooms, works of art.

The huge garden adjoining the
Malipiero-Barnabo palace on the
Grand Canal is one of the few
visible to passers-by, albeit
fleetingly from the deck of a
vaporetto, across from the Ca'
Rezzonico. Flute players and
other eighteenth-century allegorical statues meditate there; Nep-
tune keeps watch from the middle
of his temple (above). He is the
work of the sculptor Antonio
Bonazza, who created the garden's other figures as well.

The Malipiero-Barnabo palace garden was extended in the nineteenth century when a small outbuilding was torn down. Now, water, earth, stone, and flowers trade their secrets and their spells. A romantic young woman awaits a tryst beneath an ivy-covered pergola.

wasser, who owns a home on Giudecca. "One must not garden, but rather let nature do it. Allow spontaneous vegetation. Let everything grow and cut nothing. . . . It is urgent that we enter into dialogues with our gardens, that we sign peace treaties." And in fact his garden (and his remarks) obviously reflect our modern ecological sensibility—even though Giudecca, like the Lido, has traditionally hosted Venice's vegetable and pleasure gardens. There was always plenty of room, so that one could, and still can to some extent, let nature take its course.

But I'm not convinced that we must always let nature take its course. Venice was built against nature, against water, against mud, against all reason. Venice's gardens are not natural. Rebuilt in the seventeenth century, palazzo Malipiero-Barnabo is flanked by a wonderful garden (visible from the vaporetto) that looks as much like an extension of the building as it does a counterpoint to its mineral order. Weeds mix with eighteenth-century Baroque allegorical statues. One imagines an amorous tryst with a Venetian of flesh, blood, and wit, among the tea roses, flower beds, and climbing vines—or else with that other young woman, hidden beneath a pergola and sheltered by the foliage, in whose eyes of stone shines the sensual brilliance of wild goddesses. The luxuriance of plants and trees becomes an artistic effect. The landscape, in the most Romantic meaning of the word, becomes a state of mind. Water, canals, statues, blossoms, everything is organized and domesticated; only feelings remain untamed.

Venice's gardens were hard-won by their owners, who sometimes tore down houses for them. Could one imagine such a policy anywhere else in the world? The beautiful Albrizzi garden is a perfect example. A theater once stood there, San Cassiano, perhaps the first opera hall to be open to a paying public. Monteverdi was performed there, and, later, Cavalli. The theater burned down, was rebuilt, then

In the courtyard and gardens of the palazzo Giustinian, climbing plants cling to the walls, grasping the balconies, as if to help a stealthy lover reach his beloved's chamber in a Rossini opera buffa. Even the bushes are heart-shaped, capturing the amorous essence of the Serenissima.

(Above) Near the French Consulate, behind the Zattere, the terraced greenery of this sanctuary in the Giustinian-Recanati palace grounds testifies to the ingenuity of the Venetians in finding room for the pleasures of a garden within their crowded city. Note the charming "umbrella," arranged so as to protect the corner statue from the elements.

(Left) The covered altana on the roof of a house near Santa Maria Formosa. (Right) The altana of Ca' Dario, with its white linen curtains.

The secret garden that Marie Brandolini has contrived on the roof of the Giustinian palace overlooks Venice and one of the best views of the Grand Canal and the city. Gardens and statues alike are precious in Venice. In season, their protective covers are removed. From the roof terrace of this palace on the Grand Canal, one looks down over the gardens of the Ca' Dario.

This small garden behind the Querini-Stampalia palace is particularly precious to the lovers of Venice because it is not closed off for the sole pleasure of its owners, but open to the public, as are the library and the picture gallery.

In a small pool, papyrus and water lilies breathe a deliciously exotic scent into the garden. It was devised by Venetian architect Carlo Scarpa when he renovated the ground floor of the palace in the early 1960s.

A deep silence reigns, a distilled form of Oriental magic, as if Venice wanted to remind us that all its economy, history, and art came about in an ongoing exchange with the Far East.

once more fell into ruin before being bought in 1820 by the Albrizzi family, whose palace is across the rio San Cassiano. From then on, the only shows there were floral displays, for the sole benefit of the Albrizzi, who had a neo-Gothic stair tower built at its base, as well as a walkway to connect it to the *piano nobile* of their palace. The garden that replaced the theater is an exotic one, with American yuccas, rare magnolias, ferns among rocks, pools with wiggling goldfish, a pergola nestled in the wisteria.

I could cite many other examples. There is a little garden on the Zattere, not far from the French consulate, which is cultivated on a terrace. Or another garden, glimpsed through the water door of the handsome Balbi-Venier palace, where the owners, Giovanni and Charlotte Sammartini, live in an elegant apartment with delicate pastel stuccowork. This garden's grace is highlighted by the nearby Grand Canal—the palm trees' brilliant green needs the water's bronze glints and the whiteness of Istrian stone for echo and contrast. And I still enjoy seeing stone lions prowl cautiously in the shade of the garden hidden behind the ancient former chapel.

All these gardens are miraculous. Nothing favored their blossoming—their right to exist was hard-won. Ease and well-being are always tinged with merit and struggle. Idleness is a victory. Venice's gardens—gardens so well hidden they seem even unimaginable—are the ideal expressions of the obstinate, hardworking, and hedonistic genius of one of the greatest civilizations.

All gardens invite meditation, and the one behind the church of the Redentore on Giudecca is the joy of the monks who live there. A statue in the garden of a Torcello antique dealer (below). Also in Torcello, the door that opens onto the gardens of a Milanese's opulent second home.

In the calm and happy "province" of Dorsoduro, one senses its sheltered gardens and sanctuary-like-homes. There, clock hands seem to sweep a little more slowly than elsewhere. There, one has only to push open the door of a building like an abandoned factory, in corte del Sabion, to instantly enter another world: Tony Luccarda's studio.

Of course, by their very nature, all studios are enchanting. They are places not of solitude but of meeting, where artists engage in dialogues with their inspiration, their models, their chimerae. Even so, Tony Luccarda's studio is different.

The atmosphere is that of a battlefield—after the battle. It is a vast room that sculpts light and shade, a room where Venice is still; where nature palpitates as it does in the wild, out there, beyond the great glassed bays; where one smells plants, dust, and potter's clay. Most Venetian celebrities and those just passing through have visited the studio. A passionate sculptor in love with the human face, he stole a little of all their lives and their souls, kneaded it with clay (clay—Venice's basic element, half earth and half water), molded it in plaster, and cast it as silver or bronze statuettes. They have remained in detention here, those notables, or their doubles, a memory of Venice immobilized on shelves. These personalities, these faces, are everywhere, faces in plaster, potter's clay, Jivaro faces, the faces of friends—the faces that are his career. I recognize Louise de Vilmorin, discreetly elegant in a corner, not far from a severe-looking Arthur Rubinstein ("his sittings weren't much fun"). The Count Volpi and Italo Balbo seem to cohabit peaceably with a little drummer boy, the original of which was bought by Mussolini at the Venice Biennale at the end of the 1920s. I notice, up on a shelf, Ernest Hemingway's lumberjack head.

"He was living in Torcello at the time. He used to come to the studio and it was almost impossible to get him to hold still. He would drink, drag me out to

ARTISTS' HOMES, WRITERS' HOMES

The charming Quattro Fontane hotel, on the Lido, is near the casino. The owners, the sisters Pia and Bente Bevilacqua, live in a handsome private house a few meters away. The former is a painter, the latter an architect. The hotel is closed six months a year, which leaves them time to pursue their respective activities. Pia has set up a studio in a tiny lodge at the bottom of the garden, not far from the main house. Her work is greatly influenced by German expressionism.

drink with him, and then he would want to start a boxing match. Why not? But between two uppercuts, his bust would get knocked down, and I would have to start all over again. . . ."

A little farther on, Prince Xavier de Bourbon Parme appears indifferent to the beauty of a young, bare-breasted woman in a mask.

"She had the most beautiful breasts, and she knew it. She wanted her portrait done, but also wanted to remain anonymous."

Marjorie, his wife, smiles. Can one be jealous of a sculpture? Personally, I think one can. In any case, the unknown beauty remains unknown. Hemingway has taken his final bow. Rubinstein will play no more of Chopin's "Polonaises." But they all haunt Venice, inhabit Tony Luccarda's studio, and talk with him.

The youthful spirit of this man is incredible! At sixteen, he ran away from home to join D'Annunzio at Fiume and dream of heroic conquests. At twenty-five, after studying art at the Accademia in Venice, he left to seek his fortune in Paris. During World War II, he wanted nothing more than to fight on the Russian front with his regiment of royal grenadiers, but a providential double pneumonia kept him from that dubious enterprise. Tony Luccarda is a condottiere at heart, a Venetian celebrity who wears a beret or a straw hat like a helmet. He fights with an energy and a violence I could almost call "humanist" against ugliness and boredom, just to immortalize in his handsome studio a little of the worldly, seductive, cosmopolitan Venice, a little of the Venice that one loves, a little of the Venetian Venice.

No Venetian studio manages to ignore Venice, not even the attractive home of two sisters, Pia and Bente Bevilacqua, which was built at the end of the last century on the Lido, not far from Excelsior. Pia is a painter, Bente, an architect by training, and together they run the charming Quattro Fontane hotel, foun-

ded by their parents in the late 1950s. It is one of those rare hotels that give their guests the feeling of being at home, not at a hotel. Every room is a different color, with its own knickknacks and art objects. The sisters' own home nestles a few dozen meters from the hotel, at the bottom of the garden. Only the hotel cats are allowed to visit, and to enter the tiny, separate studio where Pia, influenced by Munch and the German Expressionists, creates on her canvases a violent, sometimes tragic world. The cats laze in the vast living room, into which a splendid collection of ex-votos—the oldest date from the eighteenth century—bring, even into the stairwell, a shimmering light and a beneficent protection. In her room, Bente has arranged an amusing collection of cut-out silhouettes from the Romantic era on her walls. Recognizable, among others, are Napoleon and his Grand Army officers, like Chinese shadow puppets fixed in time.

There is another Venice. It is severe, religious, hallowed in mystery, with a nearly tragic sensuality, and is to be found at Marco del Re's, across from the church of the Carmini. There, he says, he paints "with his back to history, facing new horizons." Is it possible, especially in Venice? It is not enough to turn one's back on the street, on the canals, on the Scuola

Bente has hung Romantic-era cutout silhouettes in her room. In the stairwell a splendid collection of Italian ex-votos is displayed. The oldest date from the seventeenth century. The landing receives light from this winter garden veranda, which is ideal for reading.

Artists' studios often perch under roofs at the tops of houses. Across from the church of the Carmini, to which it pensively turns its back, the dim ground floor of a house was Marco del Re's choice. The mail carrier drops letters through the slot in the front door. The wicker basket

that receives them may connote disdain for the urgency of current events, or it may be an ironic, elegant wink, a touch of beauty, simplicity, and humor in everyday life.

The world seems distant and muffled in Marco del Re's rustic studio. It opens onto a small garden filled with a profound silence— Venice suddenly appears far away.

del Carmine's Tiepolos, and to hole up in one's studio. Majestic Venetian *torchères* accompany you down the long hallway to that studio. How ought one to interpret such lighting? Nor do the smells of turpentine and linseed oil, and the cheerful profusion of brushes, rags, and charcoal pencils in the studio entirely mask the Venetian violence of the place—a humid, wintery place, strongly reminiscent of a mine's subterranean galleries, as one art critic wrote. This is something of an exaggeration, as it ignores the gracious, thickly wooded little garden that brightens and softens the painter's studio. Is he really turning his back to history, when the color that dominates his visionary frenzy is . . . carmine? Venice, too, is a fantastic land of overwhelming sensuality.

The charm of Giovanni Soccol's home clearly lies in the constant back-and-forth between past and present, which is possible only because of his fervent love for Venice and for the arts. The painter, architect-decorator, and professor at the Venice School of Fine Arts built his apartment and studio on the top floor of a house near campo San Polo, choosing—unlike Marco del Re—to capture all the light of the Venetian sky and put it into his paintings.

The absence of movement—or a taste for retirement—suits a writer's house. "Books are the

Giovanni Soccol's often visionary painting multiplies the effect of perspective. (Right) On an easel, one of his most recent works, Basilica. Early-eighteenth-century wood angels from Venezia frame the door to his studio. A Polynesian statue on a chest goes well with the curious weathervane off a boat from Chioggia. A collection of bottles from Murano (below) looks as if it were placed under the protection of a gilded horse's skull.

In his quiet Dorsoduro retreat, sculptor Tony Luccarda is looked after by his wife, Marjorie. For more than half a century he has seen nearly all the celebrities of Venice, or those visiting Venice, go by—including Hemingway, Louise de Vilmorin, Arthur Rubinstein—and he has captured them in delicate little busts, of which he keeps copies as reminders. "I am fascinated by the human face," he likes to say. His visitors, however, are fascinated by the peaceful serenity of his workplace, which is bathed in a delicate, aquarium-like light entering through large, glassed-in bays.

products of solitude and the children of silence," Marcel Proust said. Is that why the Venetian civilization—so noisy in its glittering, resonant, collective frivolities—has begotten relatively few poets, writers, and philosophers? Or to put it another way: the Venetian civilization never really enjoyed abstract speculation, and never gave rise to an intellectual elite inclined to poetry, for example, as in Florence.

So writers' houses are all the more precious in Venice. In those homes, as nowhere else, one feels very far from Venice. One feels more than the usual respect inspired by desks or book-lined libraries, something more powerful and distinct. That something is precisely the contrast between Venice's opulent and giddy beauty and the peaceful gravity of these interiors where the world suddenly trades the spectacle for a book.

I see proof of this in Carpaccio's paintings at the Scuola di San Giorgio degli Schiavoni. His exterior paintings, such as the triumph of Saint George or Saint Jerome and the miracle of the lion, are full of a surging, motley, animated life. They are Venice showing off, with its fanfares, sumptuously-attired notables, and splendid, transparent luminosity. One finds solitude and silence, on the other hand, in the "writer's house" and in Saint Jerome's scholarly monastic retreat. Suddenly, movement ceases. Carpaccio focused on the great empty spaces that fill the hermit's cell, between his books on shelves on the left and his scientific measuring instruments on the right. A kind of eternity dominates the painting, in contrast with the Venetian painter's munificent exteriors.

I received a similar impression from the large house of the writer Pier Antonio Quarantotti Gambini, who died in 1965. His wonderfully courteous brother and sister live there today. The house was originally the *ridotto* of the now-vanished San Cassiano theater. A *ridotto* is a place of pleasure, gaming, encounters (the

Writer Pier Maria Pasinetti is a native Venetian and faithful to the Dorsoduro neighborhood that inspired the settings and characters of many of his novels. Today, he divides his life between Venice and Los Angeles, where he is a university professor teaching six months a year.

etymology seems to come from *ridursi*, "to gather")—very Venetian, indeed! And yet, a writer's presence has transformed everything here: the eighteenth-century stuccowork and paintings, the freshness of the oleanders that one imagines in the garden. There is nothing sad, melancholy, or disturbing in these great rooms, where the author of *La Rosa rossa* and *La Regate di San Francisco* wrote until his death. You feel only a sort of peaceful, serene wisdom. There is a dusky happiness in prowling around the library, that silent memorial to the world. A manuscript still lies on a table, a penholder, a statuette, a pipe (it belonged to the great Triestine poet Umberto Saba, a friend of Quarantotti Gambini, himself an Istrian who moved to Venice after the war). Everything reminds us of the presence of a man, an author, someone who is departed, but not in sorrow, just with that happy recollection that one feels far from life's carnival pleasures.

I like that word, "recollection." It comes to mind at Pier Maria Pasinetti's, between the Accademia and San Barnaba, because he "collected" Venice and his Dorsoduro neighborhood in novels such as *Rosso veneziano*, *Il Ponte dell' Accademia*, and *Dorsoduro*.

It also comes to mind at the home of Peter Lauritzen, who, with his British wife, Lady Rose, moved to Venice twenty-two years ago, into the *piano nobile* of the palazzo Da Silva, in Cannaregio, which backs onto the old ghetto. A noted historian of the Serenissima, Lauritzen chose the most austere, least touristed *sestiere* in which to study, work, write and escape the present. "You don't come to Venice looking for the twentieth century," he told me, and that is indisputable. One certainly won't find the twentieth century at his house. Even his red parrot, in a cage overlooking a fine, eighteenth-century terrazzo, refers back, in its way, to the Venetians' traditional love of pets to which all their painting testifies.

A historian of Venice, Peter Lauritzen (right) moved into the piano nobile of the Da Silva palace, built in the sixteenth century. The palace was originally a casa d'affitto, that is, a house built to be rented, readily taken by ambassadors. Lauritzen perhaps wanted to enter into the spirit of the city and share the tastes and whims of the former citizens of the Serenissima. For centuries, Venetians have been known for their love of domesticated animals, particularly parrots.

Writer and journalist Riccardo Calimani (above) recently published a history of the Venice ghetto, a significant topic, given the extent to which the Jewish community and the State of Venice worked together during both their histories. In effect, the Serenissima invented the principle of the ghetto, offering refuge not only to Jews, but to other communities as well, among them Armenians, Greeks, and Turks. Alone among the Catholic states, this tolerant city never condemned anyone to death for heresy. Needless to say, however, Venice cashed in on this protection. In the eighteenth century, the city's repeated demands drove the Jewish community to bankruptcy. Its ruin led soon after to Venice's own.

The former ridotto, or game room, of the San Cassiano theater, now destroyed, was home to writer Pier Antonio Quarantotti Gambini from 1945 until his death twenty years later. Today, his brother and sister live there. (Above) The great bookcase-desk used by Pier Antonio's father, an historian. A statuette of Mercury, a bust of Dante, a collection of Bohemian glasses . . . The atmosphere in this vast room is one of peace and scholarly contemplation, despite the frivolity of the eighteenth-century wall treatment.

Alvise Quarantotti Gambini (far left), like his brother, novelist Pier Antonio, a Knight of Malta, maintains this apartment as a memorial where his brother's books, correspondence, and archives are very carefully conserved. The morning room (top, right), with its beautiful eighteenth-century stuccowork, holds many souvenirs: the photograph of the writer over the fireplace and family portraits on the walls. The desk of the writer has remained just as it was the day he died (above, right). The foliage of the San Cassiano garden rustles beyond the windows, but there is nothing inanimate or melancholic in this peaceful home, with its Pompeian frescoes (left) and floor of classic terrazzo alla veneziana. The portrait of a little girl in a sitting room (above, left), adds a charmingly fresh note.

odern interior in Venice, that city of the past, that museum-city? The architect Cristiano Gasparetto responds to this doubt spiritedly, and with at least as much passion for his city as for his profession:

"It's quite simple. We preserved everything we can preserve. But I don't agree that Venice is a city of the past. We have to preserve and devise a new plan that is compatible with the past. *That's* modernity! But above all no mimicry! Our words, our clothes, our language, our life, everything is different today. How can we not take that into account? My house does no violence to the past. I've kept what could be kept."

His house is a sober, redbrick, middle-class Venetian edifice, probably from the late seventeenth century, on the Fondamenta dei Soccorso, between campo dei Carmini and Ca' Zenobio (the word *soccorso*, "aid," refers no doubt to the Serenissima's policy of making lodgings available to needy couples or individuals). What did he keep?—only the walls and the framework. Gasparetto designed everything else: the proportions of the rooms, the decorative elements, the materials, the staircase, the attic mezzanine where he set up his office. He even designed some of the furniture. Just the same, there is another presence here as well, that of his onetime teacher, the great architect Carlo Scarpa. His influence is evident, for example, in the metal niches that define the partitions and in the living room's central fireplace, designed as an homage to the master, with its bright colors and interlocking circles. Nearby is a wooden chair inspired by a Rietveld model, with a 1920s Bauhaus feeling, while the apartment's bright colors—blue, white, and red—provide the lively contrasts of a Mondrian painting.

What makes this house Venetian is its festive air, its luminous fantasy, but mainly the materials Gasparetto used. He is proud of his use of *marmorino*, a mixture of lime, marble powder, linseed oil, and fish

MODERN STYLE

Architect Cristiano Gasparetto designed, drafted, and oversaw the renovation of his home and studio, across from the rio dei Carmini, in what was a solid bourgeois house in the late 1700s. Gasparetto believes that the modern spirit must not do violence to the past. The curved wall of the shower space (above) is made of light blue marmorino, a mixture of lime and marble, the secret of which was rediscovered by Palladio. In the dining room (opposite), the frank seductiveness of two fine Russian paintings from the 1920s harmonizes with the pure geometry of the shapes and niches designed by the owner.

glue, to which one can add colored pigments.

"Marmorino breathes," the architect explains. "It's ideal for damp places. Palladio was the first to rediscover and adopt this technique, which the Egyptians had discovered thousands of years before."

Gasparetto is obviously a true Venetian. He could talk for hours about all the techniques his ancestors used to build their city. He tells me why brick and lime withstand humidity, and how Carlo Scarpa reinvented *calce spatolata*, a spreadable lime mixture that dries as a black-dotted surface. One feels a love for Venice beating in his home, in which geometry is tempered with the intangible, unangular Venetian softness of living.

It is hard to modernize in Venice. The Office of Fine Arts watches over the city with scrupulous and very praiseworthy vigilance—one barely has the right to move an ashtray on a table! It is impossible to drive a nail into a wall, let alone move a dividing wall, without obtaining a sheaf of authorizations. But the Parma decorator and antiques dealer Carlo Medioli had none of these difficulties in his apartment in the Ca' Bernardo, a fifteenth-century palace near San Polo, because he moved into what was once the attic. There was nothing to either preserve or change—he had to create everything. He found strange harmonies between ancient and modern, between the Neoclassical spirit and Art Deco, giving a kind of severity, austerity, and sobriety to this city where nothing is really severe, austere, or sober.

Two principles governed the decoration of his apartment. First, white paint everywhere to erase borders, corners, recesses, and edges in this attic living space until it is difficult to know where the roof starts, the wall ends, and the floor disappears. Is this inconsistent with multicolored Venice? Perhaps—but isn't white the totality of all colors? Second, the little furniture and few objects that are not built into walls

Cristiano Gasparetto speaks with undisguised pride of his fireplace (opposite), designed as a tribute to his maestro, Venetian architect Carlo Scarpa. Two red lacquered wood chairs, after a Rietveld model, suggest the Bauhaus feeling of the 1920s; a floor of large terra-cotta tiles is maintained with linseed oil. Good Venetian that he is, Gasparetto always plays with light and colors in a holiday spirit. Over the dining room table (above), the attic mezzanine where Gasparetto has placed his studio and office space.

An antique dealer and decorator in Parma, Carlo Medioli created an apartment for himself in the attic of a fifteenth-century palace near campo San Polo. It's a refuge and a place to show off his best finds in an Art Deco setting. (Above) A marble neoclassic statuette. To its left, a small cherry wood temple stands out against a wall as immaculately white as the floor. Farther back, in baroque gilded wood frames, three small paintings of deities against a black background, in the Pompeian style, after the fashion of Antonio Canova. Medioli, however, is particularly proud of his collection of eighteenth-century medallions of Roman emperors (right), recently purchased from a Venetian family.

Carlo Medioli's morning room is also in the style of the 1925–1930 period, conveyed in the lines of its armchairs, upholstered in a black and white fabric. Particularly outstanding, though, is the large Art Deco table (above, right) designed by the architect Meneghetti.

The shot-and-reverse-shot effect of the two photographs above emphasizes the impression of a movie set (a film by Antonioni, perhaps), a set whose modernism is intensified by antique and retro accents.

The piano nobile of a seventeenth-century palace not far from the Rialto is unrecognizable in the apartment of art publisher Cleto Munari, as transformed by architect and decorator Ettore Sottsass. The door (above) in a black and white marble checkerboard pattern opens into the dining room. The cabinet at the back of the dining room (above, right) is partly built into the wall. The objects displayed there are designed by Ettore Sottsass and distributed by Cleto Munari. At the other end of the large living room, once the portego of the palace, one notes (right) a curious bookcase-desk surmounted by four halogen lamps with their light-diffusing glass discs. The same bookcase acts as a bar on the other side.

164

The sky-blue door of the por-tego (above, right), its white lacquered wood cornices vaguely evoking a pagoda, gives access to the kitchen (above, left). In the portego, Cleto Munari sits on a neo-Biedermeier sofa, inspired by Austrian railway waiting room benches of the 1920s and 1930s.

Munari says of the apartment: "Everyone I've shown it to has liked it very much, except my wife. She hasn't quite accepted it, because she prefers coordinated colors—brown with beige, for example. But Sottsass matched brown with violet, green, sky-blue. A whole rainbow!"

or floor seem to float in his house—an effect unsettling in the extreme.

Cleto Munari, goldsmith and maker of art objects and limited-edition jewelry, may be more Venetian in spirit than in his official address, since he works and lives mostly in Vicenza. The keynote of his apartment on the *piano nobile* of a seventeenth-century palace, between San Polo and the Rialto, is "tour de force." For the decoration, he gave Ettore Sottsass, a friend for more than twenty-five years, carte blanche. "It seemed to me," Munari said, "that he had the perfect ability to identify with the Venetian atmosphere and still stay totally modern."

Modern, indeed. Cleto Munari wasn't disappointed. The vast *portego* with its long, neo-Biedermeier divan and odd pale-wood central desk containing books, records, and stereo equipment; the black-and-white checkerboard door frames; the built-in, stepped, combination sideboard and storage unit. . . . The ruling motifs are severity, astonishment, invention, and decoration—even gaudiness, in the best sense of the word. And that is perfectly in keeping with the city of Venice, itself so entirely, nobly, sumptuously gaudy.

Although Flavio Albanese sometimes decorates houses in New York, he, too, is a full-fledged spiritual citizen of the Serenissima. He, too, says that Venice must not sink under the weight of the past, but his attic apartment in a little house in campo San Maurizio, scented with the smells of cakes from the delicious Marchini pastry shop downstairs, sinks under what one could call Venice's aquatic charms. For Flavio Albanese has had made for his home (the former Scuola degli Albanesi, where Carpaccio is said to have worked) small gold mosaic tiles, which he used to form on the floor lines that distantly recall the water patterns of the city.

Architect and decorator Flavio Albanese seems to have been guided by a single certainty in renovating this little apartment in a house near campo San Maurizio: Venice is a city bathed in light. This hallway (right) is as fluid as a Venetian rio. The flooring is a mosaic of paste tesserae that changes color with the daylight, like the waters of the lagoon. In a display cabinet (below), a collection of contemporary Murano glasses signed by Venini. And because Venice is also the glittering city, the city of gold, the decorator has wittily gilded a metal beam that supports blue-coated neon lighting (above).

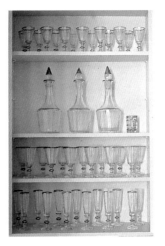

166

Flavio Albanese designed this couch covered in a linen-cotton blend and obviously finds it comfortable. On a pedestal table (left), also designed by him, a Barovier-Toso vase from the 1940s. On another small table (right), Venini glasses stand out against the linen screens that shade the windows. Louis-Philippe chairs (opposite) are arranged on the lagoon colors of the mosaic floor. Flavio Albanese's style has been likened to Carlo Scarpa's. They share a taste for sparse decoration, a pleasure that becomes a kind of delightful sensuality.

What could a huge, middle-class, chalet-style house on the Lido, an old rural shack surrounded by a vegetable garden on Torcello, and *casoni* lost at the end of their *valli* have in common? Just this: these houses have fled Venice for the lagoon, and thus benefit from the privilege of space. Outside are light, water, grounds for play, fishing, hunting, growing things, strolling. But inside, too, space is ample. No longer a luxury as it is in Venice, where one is always comparing the size of the most luxurious palaces with the narrowness of the humblest homes, here it is simply one's due. These houses are not luxurious, they display no outward sign of wealth. On the contrary, they are houses that hide. One comes to live here when one has had enough of the world and the business of Saint Mark's Square. One comes here to get away and find another, perhaps more intimate kind of happiness.

I have experienced this well-being on Torcello, for example. Not so much in the idyllic Locanda Cipriani, where presidents of the French Republic, British princesses, and Hollywood stars sometimes retire in the perfect illusion of rustic happiness. And not so much in the luxurious second homes tucked away on the island, nor even in the beautiful antiquary by the cathedral, its garden seemingly strewn with ancient statues and capitals. I have experienced this well-being in the modest peasant home of two brothers, practically adjoining the *locanda* on the canal. In the soothing dimness of their home, they restore old paintings. They work to consolidate the past, possessed by a kind of resignation that is tinged not with sadness but something else, the indifference of those who have chosen to make their homes on the outer edges of life and of current events. The two brothers are out of step with the present, indifferent to progress, and entirely astonished at receiving visitors. In fact, they seem to sum up the life of Torcello, along the lagoon that man has given up taming, stopped

ON THE LAGOON

In the southern part of the lagoon, the valle Zappa is one of the most beautiful, and the richest in wildlife. The vast and picturesque cason Zappa, in the Scandinavian Gothic style, was built in 1925–1928, according to plans by the architect Torres. On a table, handsome painted wood decoys.

fighting to keep himself on the crest of the present. Then, the only perspective left is memory, the only reason to live and breathe, patience.

It is impossible to write about the houses of the lagoon without ending with a word on the *casoni*, lost at the bottom of their *valli*. The *casoni* comprise several different structures: the residence; the shed for storing work, fishing, or hunting gear; the boat house; and finally the workshop where the boat is maintained or repaired. In addition, the *casoni di caccia* often have a small tower, which one climbs a few days before a hunting party to observe the birds' movements.

Outside, the lagoon palpitates with its most teeming, secret life. It prowls and encircles the house. The lagoon is everywhere, swampy, labyrinthine, almost unsettling, overflown by wild ducks. Buried in the *casoni*, one feels a little bit imprisoned in the lagoon— a delightful feeling. As a result, the atmosphere is warm, intimate, comfortable, rustic, and peaceful. The walls are often paneled with oak planks or rushes, decorated with hunting souvenirs and brightened with many-colored decoys. Nature becomes fixed, its flesh-and-blood birds become wooden birds. A comforting thought indeed. The art of living in Venice also encompasses winter weekends far out on the lagoon, where a pretty room with a brass bed is enough, and one doesn't consider the recent, superfluous installation of electricity to be important progress, where once methane lamps gave light.

The hunters or anglers return, enlivening the house. Many *casoni* have, adjoining the living room, an odd sort of fireplace room with a central hearth. Even before taking off boots or oilskin, we warm ourselves around it in winter. Later, we will grill sea-perch there, to be enjoyed with the inevitable polenta. The smoke that wafts from under the hood promises a feast, a simple pleasure only the true Venetians know and share.

The animal skins and stuffed
birds in the great vestibule of the
cason Zappa recall the hunt, the
main activity—with fish-
breeding—of those who live on
the lagoon.

In a casone, the traditional fire-place room (far left), where people gather after hunting or fishing. Another room (left), with carved wood furniture.

Two brothers, picture-restorers, live in this rustic little house on Torcello. The perfectly preserved kitchen is not at all "designed." Everything has its place—brass pots, oven, hanging lamp, and the wood table weathered by the years. Here, beauty derives from tradition unselfconsciously preserved. A country happiness reigns in their house, seemingly very far from the Serenissima's restlessness, luxury, and splendid whirl. Time unfolds at a different speed.

How does one rejuvenate and strengthen the past, or restore light and beauty to works of art? It is less a question of technique than of philosophy. The two brothers capture the past in their house on Torcello, with its old brick stove and vegetable garden at the bottom of which flows the canal.

The hurried tourist who lands on Torcello to visit the basilica will miss this house, contiguous with the Locanda Cipriani. It is surrounded by a vast garden; its brick wall sports stone bas-reliefs; it seems an oasis of calm and serenity. This is Torcello's captivating charm, for those who take the time to explore its geography and imagine its history.

Long ago, around A.D. 1000, Torcello was the most prosperous and populated island of the lagoon. Today, it numbers only about one hundred inhabitants, most of whom—like the picture-restorer brothers and their elderly mother (left)—passionately tend their vegetable gardens.

Opening onto the dining room in this casone is the fireplace room in which one can warm oneself before a luncheon of grilled fish. A bouquet of dried flowers is arranged on an armchair in front of the window (above) On the lagoon, sky, land, and water are in harmony; so, in the casoni, are the warm golden tones of woods, reeds, and flowers.

Nestled at the ends of the lagoon's meanders are houses—the casoni—lost in the marshy, maze-like landscape. These houses are often used as hunting or fishing lodges. They are rustically furnished: wood prevails, and reeds on the walls; decoys are decorative elements. They are perhaps the secret heart of Venice—or at least the native Venetians' weekend retreats, especially in hunting season. Retreats, indeed: only regulars can find them, only the true Venetians know the lagoon's labyrinths, the shifting play of its channels and its shallows. At night, they may even venture to row home, taking their bearings from the water's scent, which changes with the depth.

Bread and cheese—with polenta,
a country lunch. These sim-
plicities contrast sharply with the
luxury and refinement that sometimes surround the life of these
same patricians once they return
to the palaces of Venice.

TRADITIONS

Discussions of the Serenissima's earliest history usually emphasize the commercial genius of its citizens, their progress along the river, then the sea routes; the sprawling way in which, from the tenth century on, they expanded their trading routes into the Far East. They traded in cloth, spices, slaves, saints' relics—anything that might show a profit—with absolute cynicism. They lived thus for centuries, moved solely by the lure of money, to the point where their rapacity shocked the rest of the Christian world. But to reduce Venice to banking or commerce, to imagine even for a moment that Venice produced nothing in its history but "merchants," would be bizarrely shortsighted. In fact, during its first stage (for simplicity's sake, from 1400 to 1800) the Republic of Venice survived thanks only to its artisans. At the time, the city teemed with tanners, blacksmiths, jewelers, weavers, armorers, glassmakers, porcelain manufacturers, wood-and-ivory-carvers, organ builders, playing-card makers, and many, many others.

What precisely do they make? I say they make mostly souvenirs of Venice. The most wretched colored-glass knickknack from Murano and the finest embroidered linen for sale in the vast Jesurum showroom at Ponte della Canonica in the nave of the former Sant' Apollinia church, both are defined first by the magical, key word *Venice*. After all, that's what Canaletto was doing in the eighteenth century when he turned out views of the Grand Canal or the Saint Mark's Basin. What were they but luxury postcards for the rich British tourist who, his painting under his arm, would return home and think of Venice for the rest of his days? I remember one of Ernst Lubitsch's most irresistible comedies, *Trouble in Paradise*. In the first scene, the pickpocket Herbert Marshall robs Edward Everett Horton in a swank hotel room in Venice. A few months later, in Paris, the two men are formally introduced, and poor Horton asks himself

The art of bookmaking—of printing and papermaking—is one of the most respected of the many crafts in which Venetian artisans excel. Puncheons and gold leaf for gold tooling a book at the Ex Libris bindery (above).

(Preceding pages) A bronze head in the ancient style from Luigi Valese's workshops. When one thinks of Venetian art, one conjures up the eighteenth century and the luminous, brilliant genius of the great stuccoworkers— Giuseppe Boccanegra keeps this illustrious tradition alive. For three generations, the Boccanegras have been creating or restoring the stuccowork of the finest Venetian structures, in particular the renovations in the palazzo Grassi. (Right) Several plaster models of Boccanegra stuccowork are arranged on a sort of wood tabernacle.

where the devil he has met this guy before. He draws on his cigarette, then crushes it into a . . . gondola-shaped ashtray. It all comes back! Glass gondolas are made on Murano so that one will remember Venice. The artisans of Venice make glasses, plates, embroidered handkerchiefs, velvets, and furnishing fabrics. They create and export splinters, pieces of their city, so that one will never stop dreaming of Venice.

I have never seen any of them exhibit the slightest merchant's obsequiousness. Shopkeepers are neither contemptuous, haughty, arrogant, nor offensive. They merely maintain the discretion and courtesy of people who are aware—however intuitively or unconsciously—that they represent more than just themselves, that they are heirs to an entire body of knowledge, an entire tradition. In a word, an entire civilization.

Just after the war, a young Venetian woman was amazed by the odd hours the artisans' shops were open. They might be closed during the day, but one could walk in very late on a summer night. She had discovered a sign, hanging on the window of a small silversmith, that said, in Venetian dialect: *Verzo co vogio, sero co vogio* ("I open when I want, I close when I want"). I myself have never seen such a sign anywhere. On reflection, however, I wouldn't be surprised to see it on the door of the Sfrisos' shop, on the little campo San Tomà. The two brothers, Giancarlo and Professor Mario Sfriso, are perfectly aware that, for them, the world of goldsmithing ended with the age of Benvenuto Cellini. They work gold and silver with the same kinds of gravers and chasing chisels, and ewers, plates, and goblets emerge from their hands. Naturally, they do not only imitate the old, but also create new designs for use or decoration as their father did before them. Their workroom, where they work for hours on end, is behind their shop. I have spent long, companionable moments with Professor Mario Sfriso, chatting about Paris, his international

The vast goldsmithy (above) of the brothers Giancarlo and Mario Sfriso is in campo San Tomà, behind the showroom and shop. They like to say that, for them, time stopped with Benvenuto Cellini. But was the great Florentine goldsmith of the Renaissance familiar with the soldering iron? (Right) Professore Giancarlo Sfriso finishes a small silver gondola.

Several plaster casts of the antique-style pieces in the Sfriso brothers' repertoire. Each piece is unique, hand-engraved with tools that have remained virtually the same for centuries: chasing chisels, small steel scissors, pliers, pincers, tiny hammers. A silver ewer in a classical style (above, right). "There is no limit of shape or process to what we can produce," Mario Sfriso says. But for him and his brother, gold and silver are still the noblest materials, the ones they most enjoy working.

In the Cannaregio neighborhood, between the Madonna dell'Orto and the Casinò degli Spiriti, at the north end of the lagoon, is Luigi Valese's foundry. This family firm has been making ornamental objects in bronze and brass since 1918: door knockers, key chains (top, right: the Hotel Connaught's in London), door-

knobs, madonnas (right), light fixtures, and their specialty, the little horses that adorn the sides of gondolas. Once, each family had its own model of bronze cavallo, and, even today, Valese produces about fifty different ones. The fine sand that fills his molds comes from the Fontainebleau forest.

At Luigi Valese's workshop, there reigns an industrious atmosphere and a respect for tradition—the pieces are cast one after another by hand. On Thursdays and Fridays, Valese and his five workers process the mixture of zinc and copper for the casting of different pieces of brass. The other days of the week, the pieces are polished, filed, readied to be sold.

cliental, and the other great goldsmiths that he admires. Once the ice was broken, he was willing to divulge the secrets of his art. The shop could wait, the customers would come back.

"I open when I want, I close when I want" is a profession of faith I unhesitatingly attribute to Crea, whose *squero*, or shipyard for gondolas was situated, until a recent fire, at the very end of Venice, beyond Sant' Elena. They do not welcome every passing idler. German shepherds prowl among the workbenches and the skeletons of the craft. It's better to wait for the owner to leash them before a visit. Crea, a colossus about thirty years old, possesses a clear gaze and a sometimes daunting anger. I have heard him get up in arms about the too-passive, too-defeatist Venetians who won't take a stand for their city's survival.

"If you love Venice, you have to fight for Venice, work at Venice. It's an ongoing brawl—a city that lives only on tourism is a dead city, you understand?"

I understand, and I could easily imagine Crea's ancestors routing the Genoese, Turkish, and Barbary fleets. He has to be satisfied, less heroically, with having won Venice's most prestigious rowing race, the *Regata storica*, for years. He only trains in his spare time, but rowing is second nature to him. When he was ten, he told me, his father would take him fishing far out on the lagoon, so they would rise well before

Crea is unarguably Venice's most famous and colorful gondola-maker. The workshop employs a half-dozen artisans. An assistant (below, left) gives the last touch of paint to a gondola before delivering it to the owner. Crea also makes the forcole *(above), those strange, splendid, and functional supports that hold the oar.*

dawn. He would row in the bow, saying over and over, "I want to sleep!" "Learn to lean on the oar, learn to sleep while you row," his father would reply.

Today, Crea not only rows, but makes oars, *forcole*, and gondolas. Indeed, he is the only one in Venice whose shipyard produces all the pieces that make up a gondola. I am suddenly reminded of a lady who lives near campo San Polo. She wouldn't miss a *Vogalonga* for the world, and swears by Renato, her mail carrier, who between his two deliveries makes, in her eyes, the most beautiful *forcole* imaginable. Crea manufactures around five or six gondolas a year. Today, gondolas rarely last more than twenty years, for the waves and the wash of motorboats wear them out prematurely. Crea the ardent, Crea the champion, Crea the Venetian doesn't care for anything that damages the beauty of his art. The evening I met him, he was burning with indignation because some Japanese industrialists had ordered a gondola that they wished to set in a pond in front of their factory's home office. Why was he so angry?

"You see, they wanted me to make the gondola half as long but just as wide, so that it could float freely in their pond. I refused, of course, but how dare they suggest such a piece of work!"

Sero co vogio, translated, "I do nothing I don't want to," was his reply to these Japanese who were a little too free and easy with the traditions of Venetian artisanry.

"Of all the arts, I know none more adventurous, uncertain, and therefore more noble than the arts that call on fire," said Paul Valéry. And of all the "fire arts," the art of glassmaking seems to be tied to Venice both historically and symbolically. The "city of light" had to shine, and it shone thanks to its master-glassmakers (and by the brilliance of the multicolored Murano glass chandeliers in all of its finest palaces). Is it generally known, for example, that eyeglasses were invented here? How does one transform such poor

Murano is not only home to master glassmakers, but to etchers on glass- and mirror-makers as well. Among the latter is the well-respected firm S.A.L.I.R. (Studio Ars et Labor Industrie Riunite), run by the cofounders' sons, Mario Dal Paos and Luigi Toso. The etched wineglass (top) with its siren design is a 1930 style by Guido Balsamo-Stella. When they are shipped, the glasses are protected with every precaution, for some are priceless. Grinders of every shape are used to cut the sheet of glass to achieve the desired ornamentation (opposite).

and lusterless materials—silica, limestone, and soda—into a glimmering surface? Here, in my opinion, is the entire history of Venice in a nutshell.

The city's genius is usually associated with the colors of Bellini, Titian, and Tiepolo. Fine. But why—to speak only of the twentieth century—are the names of artists like Ercole Barovier and Archimede Seguso regularly overlooked? It is flagrant injustice. I recall a large retrospective of the former's work at the Correr museum in 1989. I had been particularly struck by some 1930s vases of a milk-white, parchment-like transparency, with black handles and edges. I remember meeting the latter in his studio at the Fondamenta Serenella, on Murano. Now over eighty, Seguso is still unquestionably the most illustrious living master-glassmaker. His pieces fetch record prices in the great auction rooms. He has never ceased inventing techniques for blending gold into glass or creating new forms of filigree. Like all the great master-glassmakers, he guards his secrets and his discoveries jealously. But Archimede Seguso impressed me above all because I saw him as the epitome of the history of Venice. His family's tradition of glassmaking can be traced to the sixteenth century. Archimede's great-grandfather was one of the architects of the industry's renaissance in the second half of the nineteenth century, and appears in D'Annunzio's *Il Fuoco* in the character of the prince of the *Maestri Vetrai.* Prince for prince, Archimede seemed to me truly royal. Seated on a shabby stool in his workshop, he didn't have to say a word to be understood—a brief gesture, a glance, the tap of pincers on the leg of his seat, these were enough. His two sons have carried out the firm's commercial expansion and multiplied its outlets in Italy and abroad. As for him, with the modesty or the laconic pride of wise old men, he is content to stay on his high stool and work, invent, and provide Venice with its most astonishing transparencies when light awakens the gleam of gold leaf in

(Above, left) The great grinder for polishing glass. Etched flagons and, behind them, the rack where the different grinders are kept (above, right). A machine for polishing pieces of mirrors (left), with its polishing powder . . . and everywhere the spirit of artistry that arises from the most ancient traditions.

(Above, left) A Venetian mirror ready for packing. The firm can make more than one thousand different styles of mirrors, with fretwork frames cut from carefully preserved templates (left). (Above, right) A detail of a rough-cut frame.

glass or turns air bubbles iridescent. I asked him how long it had taken to make the vase he held in his hand. He answered: "More than six hundred years."

There are others who could say the same. It has taken centuries upon centuries for everything that Venice continues to make—and to invent—today. Also on Murano, the firm of S. A. L. I. R. etches and decorates glass (not of its own manufacture) following very old traditions. In the northern part of Cannaregio, between the Madonna dell' Orto and the Casino degli Spiriti, facing the lagoon and San Michele Island, there are still, side by side, more or less renovated workshops and factories black with coal dust, patina, and, I might add, human sweat.

One glacial winter day (blissfully interrupted by frequent stops in small cafés of the Fondamenta dei Mori, where "Cannaregians" play cards for hours at a stretch, and where I drank expresso after espresso, dunking *fritelle*, those large raisin- or pine-nut-stuffed fritters prepared at Carnival time), I met a sailmaker who redesigned sails for the older models of Venetian boats, and the last bronze-founder in Venice, Valese, out of whose workshop came sirens, fabulous beasts, horses for the sides of gondolas, and key rings for the

Bevilacqua fabrics are still woven on eighteenth-century Jacquard looms. The price of this "Pavoni" silk velvet (opposite) is obviously in line with its splendor—about $675* a yard.

(Right) A woman spools silk threads. In the workshop's racks, the old perforated cards that "program" the fabrics' designs into the machine (left).

[*Based on 5.4 fr to the dollar 8/5/90]

196

rooms of the Danieli and the Gritti. Are these artisans representatives of a vanishing species? I dare hope they are not. . . .

But for how long will the sumptuous velvets continue to be produced, the finest silk damasks, craquelés, and brocades created by the famous Venetian firm Rubelli, or by Bevilacqua, near the little campo San Zan Degola on Santa Croce? Half a century ago, about sixty women still worked at Bevilacqua, on eighteenth-century Jacquard looms that still had their original stone counterweights. Today, there are four. Almost every manufacturer has replaced their handlooms with automated machines. On the other hand, who is willing to commit to a five-year apprenticeship that will in the end enable the weaver to stay cooped up for eight hours in order to produce, at day's end and with the help of an assistant, sixteen inches (with a width of twenty-four inches, the most a hand-loom allows) of a *velluto cisellato* or a *damasco*? (Rubelli fabrics inspire dreams, as do those of Bevilacqua, whose customers are the elite: the pope clothes his Vatican porters in their fabrics.) No other Italian city has such a manufacturer of handmade fabrics. But if, by some mischance, Bevilacqua were one day to stop its Venice production of gold-shot velvets and brocades, then I think the world would become a little duller and Venice would shine a little less brightly, like a sky in which a star has gone out.

Permanence and innovation—Venetian artisanry wavers between these two words, these two poles. Archimede Seguso likes to say: "I grew up without any particular artistic education, with no intention of becoming famous, but I have always wanted to evolve, to go farther. I have always worked to achieve the making of things I have never made before." In this goal one can see Venice's conquering, exploring tradition, as well as a city that is untiring in its will to consolidate the past, to simply keep it alive. But nothing is ever simple here. Venice, the city of high

Tapestry-maker Pasinetti restores the oldest and finest hangings. (Above) workers are busy in his workshop, and a detail of a wall hanging from the Ca' Rezzonico, currently being restored (top). This is another Venetian skill: preserving the past, maintaining its former splendor, beauty, and luxury. Various models of chairs and sofas are arranged in this room of the palace that houses the workshops. Here, the chiaroscuro prevails—that is Venice's allure and, perhaps, its magic. Pasinetti also makes sumptuous copies of antique costumes, both for the theater and for individuals at carnival time.

Troïs, a shop on the campo San Maurizio, is the sole outlet for Fortuny fabrics. On the table in the foreground, "Orsini" and "Corone" cottons. Though legend drapes Venice only in Fortuny, at carnival time the city dons a tricorn made by Amalia Marzato's shop near the Rialto. The milli-

ner creates them in every style and for any pocketbook—the most extravagant sell for about $850*.

[*Based on £1,182 to the dollar 8/5/90]

Two "historic" costumes designed by Mariano Fortuny: "Delphos," a dress of pleated silk taffeta, and its cape of silk velvet shot with gold. Marcel Proust's heroines and the beauties of the Belle Époque may have vanished forever, but the dresses of Fortuny crystallize in Venice our timeless nostalgia for bygone days.

CORSO
DI
LAVORO

ANTICA
INDUSTRIA
PATRIA

culture, is not a simple place; it requires ineffable effort and, more than effort, genius, if it is to go on shining. Were it not for the excellence of its artisans, Venice would be a dead star. I am thinking of a very young man like Michele Cicogna, who, on campo San Tomà just across from the Sfriso goldsmithy, restores antique paintings and furniture, as his father and his grandfather did before him. The application of gold leaf, varnishes, and lacquers no longer holds secrets for him. When I visited, he was restoring a delicate painting of a Chinese man on his dromedary on eighteenth-century polychrome doors from the Ca' Rezzonico. He acted as magician, erasing the wear of years.

As for the art of lacemaking, there is no question of past or present, but only of eternity. What is an hour, two hours, dozens or hundreds of hours to make a bedspread in a flat Venice point, or a handkerchief edged in lace of the Burano school, with its blocks, stripes, and miniscule *point d'esprit*? Vermeer captures the right mood in his *Lacemaker*. It is a metaphysical art, defying the miseries of time with the beauty and perfection of the useless. It is a lesson in wisdom.

I believe lacemaking is typically Venetian as well. History tells us that point lace was invented by Venetian needlewomen in the 1540s. The genius of their innovation lay in no longer drawing threads through the piece to be embroidered, but in constructing the grid, or framework, for their work themselves. It is

At the Burano museum, one can admire the detail that made the lace of Venice famous (opposite). The embroidered linen tablecloth trimmed with nineteenth-century Venetian lace (opposite, bottom left) comes from the Jesurum collections, and represents approximately three years' work. On Burano, each piece of lace requires the work of seven workers, from the designer to the finisher. The panel above was made by a student at the lace school after two years of study. It took her six hundred hours.

the spirit of lace that is especially Venetian. At once virginal and erotic, it stands for luxury, sensual pleasures, and the play of semblances. And, once again, like Venice it defies time. Death doesn't prowl the Serenissima, as too many of the greatest writers have tediously iterated. Venice is a city where people live. Consider its great artists: Titian passed away at the age of 100, Sansovino at 93, Bellini at 86, Palma the Younger at 84, Tiepolo at 80—they all flirt with eternity. How can one die in a city where the clocks have stopped, where everything seems immutable: the Byzantine and Gothic palaces on the Grand Canal, the passing gondolas, the gaze of cats, the mother-of-pearl color of the lagoon, and the milk-white of the Burano needlework stoles.

What a strange, fantastic contrast between Burano's vivid colors and its immaculate lace! The houses of fisherfolk and artisans—bright blue, emerald green, candy pink, wisteria mauve, straw yellow—look like children's toys. On the island's main square rises the Scuola Merletti di Burano, with its austere brick facade, one of the last lacemaking schools in the world. Inside are a halfdozen seated students, their work supported on small, cylindrical, white linen pads. Outside, beyond the ogival windows, the city's colors sing and call to one another. By contrast, the luminous white of the student-lacemakers' work is like eternity's silence. I know no other beauty as secret, as unsettling as lace, which captures Venice to such a degree.

The Legatoria Piazzesi, near Sant Maria del Giglio, is a charming shop specializing in hand-printed paper. (Opposite) A sampler of their styles. Small bound boxes and motley papiermâché figurines of commedia dell'arte characters give the shop a festive air. The same spirit inhabits Ex Libris, a shop near San Polo, where they still bind books by hand (top).

Michele Cicogna, like his father and grandfather before him, restores antique furniture and paintings. In his workshop (above, left), he renews the brilliant luster of a painted door from the Ca' Rezzonico, its oriental motif recalling the art of Giovanni Battista Tiepolo. Antonio Crovato is one of the leading producers of terrazzo alla veneziana (far right). This flooring—marble chips embedded in a putty matrix—adorns practically all the palaces and

great houses of Venice. (Right) The pieces of marble are unloaded at the canal entrance. (Above, right) A series of riddles, used to sort the marble pieces, are stored at the canal entrance threshold. Crovato also follows the most ancient traditions to make pastellone, that is, powdered colored marble mixed with lime. (Opposite) Several kinds of flooring available from this artisan.

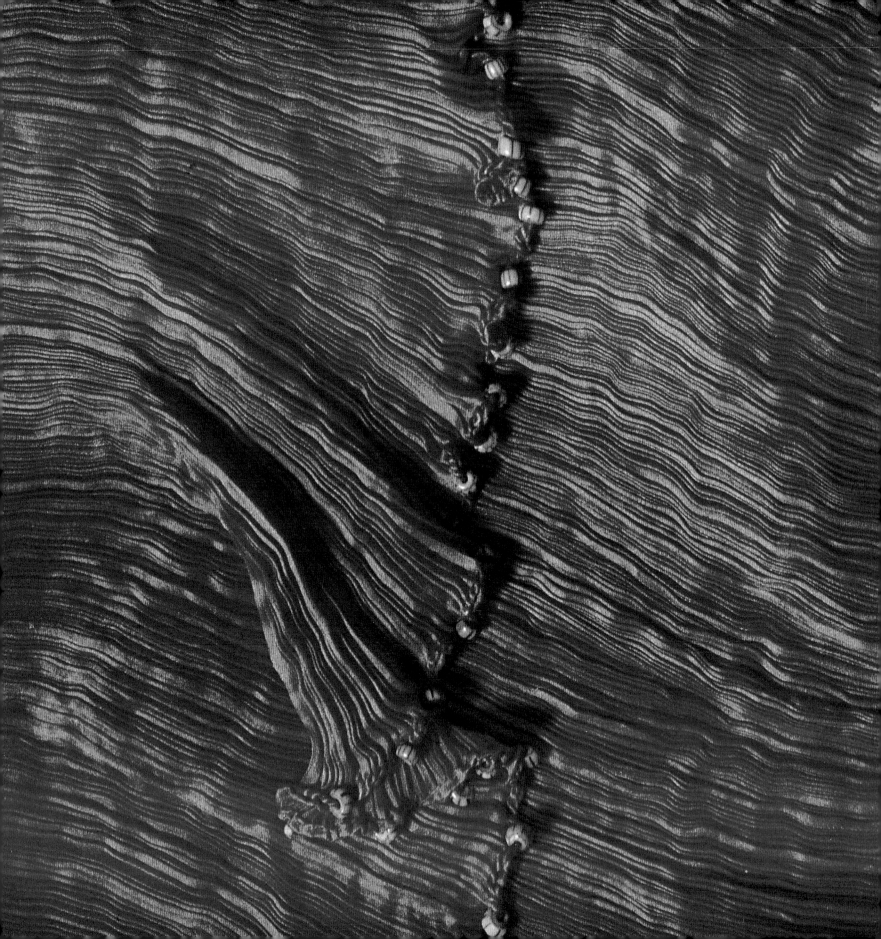

RENDEZVOUS

Venice exhibits two apparently contradictory qualities: it is both provincial and cosmopolitan. It is provincial in the manner of small towns far removed from the hectic life. There everyone knows, observes, and meets everyone else. As a city it is also cosmopolitan, a rare and wonderful capital that for almost ten centuries has been a magnet for travelers from all over the world. On the one hand, then, the calm and enchantment of the Serenissima's serene life. On the other hand, an extraordinary cultural and social openness to the world. The provincial face welcomes strangers, the cosmopolitan keeps its secrets. I know a French painter and set designer who came here thirty years ago to work on an opera set for La Fenice. He fell in love with the city, and like all passionate lovers, sacrificed his life to his passion, and never left again.

Love requires intimacy, but it is difficult to penetrate a city's intimacy when feeling like just one more tourist among a million others. One must leave the beaten paths, the crowded *calli*, the inevitable stops, the obligatory museums (but equally one must enter beneath the Byzantine cupolas of San Marco, "that pirates' cathedral, enriched by the spoils of the universe," as Théophile Gautier said). Venice is not cruel. However, one must earn it, win it, court it, learn its secrets, devine its weak points—and its strong points. Venice's intimacy lies in certain hotels, cafés, churches, junk shops, restaurants, and palaces, in short, those public places that feel so private, where one suddenly feels not like the client, but like the hotelier, not the outsider, but the guest.

Gritti, Danieli, and Cipriani are deluxe hotels, universally known passwords that connect Venice to the charms of *luxe, calme et volupté*, of legend. There is no hierarchy of passwords: one has only to recite them one after another in order to enter into Venetian rapture—that singular intoxication that goes to your head like an overdose of beauty.

The Hotel Danieli (above) is named for Giuseppe Da Niel, who in 1822 began renting rooms in the fourteenth-century former Dandolo palace. Although the interior has undergone many alterations, the Gothic facade remains untouched.

Another of the Serenissima's luxury hotels is the Cipriani on Giudecca (opposite), which charms the visitor with its vast gardens by the lagoon, its shrubbery, and the cypresses that seem to compete with the nearby campanile of San Giorgio Maggiore. (Preceding pages) Detail of "Delphos," a Fortuny dress.

I suggest a pre-lunch cocktail at the Gritti around noon, not in the intimate warmth of the bar but on the terrace by the Grand Canal, with its view opening out toward the Salute and Punta della Dogana. Yes, it looks like a postcard, but so what? It is as splendid as if one were in a Canaletto or a Guardi painting—no, one *is* there—with the white Istrian stone, bright marbles, the Sânta Maria del Giglio *traghetto*, the Byzantine-Renaissance facade of Ca' Dario across the canal, and the emerald-green water. It is Venice looking like Venice.

For lunch, head in the direction of San Marco along calle Largo XXII Marzo, then take calle Vallaresso to the right. The corner of the *fondamenta* hides the inescapable Harry's Bar, discovered by Hemingway, the home of Arrigo Cipriani's invention, the Bellini, his famous peach-juice-and-champagne cocktail. Although Harry's Bar serves some of the best food in Venice, I'm not sure that *le tout* Venice still meets there. But you see just about everyone else there, waiting in vain for the Venetian celebrities who prefer more intimate—and less expensive—meeting places. Continuing on my stroll, I leave the piazzetta and the Doges' Palace for the Riva degli Schiavoni to take the Number 5 *motoscafo* to Giudecca and Harry's Dolci's restful terrace by the water. Today, the true Venetians prefer this cheerful, light-filled annex, especially for Sunday lunches. The prices are saner, the pastries more exotic. Their tarts and cream cakes remind me sacrilegiously of the frothy, delicate, and ethereal Tiepolos of the church of the Gesuiti, whose white Rococo facade I see just across the Giudecca canal, on the Zattere.

Time passes quickly, always too quickly in Venice, where centuries stand still but days and hours tumble over one another. Dusk rises over the city. I arrive at the Danieli's upper terrace—another select view over the Saint Mark basin and the island of San Giorgio Maggiore, over stones that turn pink, water that turns

Casa Frolla (above) is among
the loveliest places to stay in
Venice. Intimate, modest, and elegant, its comforts are sometimes
summary, but its beauty is unde-
niable. It owes much of its charm
to its romantic garden, which invites ease and meditation after the
tiring whirl of visiting the city
all day. (Right) The Gritti's hospitable bar offers one of the most
impressive views of the Grand
Canal.

One can rent a small apartment in the palazzo del Giglio and admire the Baroque angels of the neighboring church in perfect privacy.

The Cipriani is famous for its cocktails—the Bellini (peach juice and prosecco—a dry, sparkling wine), the Canaletto (framboise and prosecco), the Mimosa (blood-orange juice and prosecco). Breakfast is served in the lagoon's meditative stillness.

The historic Hotel des Bains (above), its dining room patiently awaiting the season, is on the Lido. The deserted drawing room, in an Art Deco style that has come to be called "Visconti" (opposite), seems eternally ready to receive the gentlemen and veiled and parasoled Belle Époque ladies of Thomas Mann's stories.

The delightful Quattro Fontane hotel, near the casino, is an intimate, elegant retreat that recalls a rustic cottage.

Prussian blue, a sky immense as a Technicolor delirium. I confess that I am not very fond of the Danieli's medieval-style grand staircase and inner court, a popular style at the turn of the century, but I greet respectfully the ghosts I run into at every turn. Venice is not a dream-city, it simply offers two conditions that are alien to the modern spirit: calm and continuity. These alone permit the happy, I might say necessary, coexistence between the spirits of the past and the people of the present. At the Danieli, don't try to reserve Room 10; George Sand and Alfred de Musset have it. Don't be surprised if Marcel Proust is talking with Richard Wagner in one of the sitting rooms, Balzac is meditating on the human comedy in his room, or Dickens on the London slums. The hotel often has no vacancies.

Where ought one sleep in Venice? In a luxury hotel, or in one of those charming little hotels in which the Serenissima gives itself with greater abandon and heady modesty. I recall the delightful little Quattro Fontane hotel on the Lido near the Casino, and the unique beauty of each room with its painted furniture and artworks. I also recall the irreplaceable, eighteenth-century Casa Frollo on Giudecca, between the Redentore and the Zitelle, with its vegetable garden torpid in the summer heat like a paradise lost. Its rooms provide a sometimes rudimentary comfort, but the view of the Salute and the Doges' Palace is never less than royal. The furniture is old Venetian pieces (D'Annunzio is said to have passed a blazing night there with Eleanora Duse). Today, its prices are unbeatable—but will it soon be closed and turned into a deluxe hotel that will make a profit at the expense of its soul? I also recall La Fenice et des Artistes, next to the opera. There, the day after a performance of *Don Pasquale* or *Il Barbiere di Seviglia* you may exchange views with Norina or Almaviva, who are, necessarily, staying at your same hotel.

Where ought one sleep in Venice? I know at least

"Buon appetito, signori!" *The cook at the Corte Sconta, near the Arsenal, proudly displays a plateful of spider crabs (above). Later, one may take a glass of vin santo, coffee, and uvetti— raisins macerated in grappa— with the dessert cookies (right).*

Long bypassed by tourists, today the Corte Sconta is enjoying a well-deserved resurgence in popularity. Venetian specialties include spaghetti in cuttlefish ink—al nero di seppia—and squillfish. This simple and remarkable fare captures the very spirit, scent, and flavor of Venice and its lagoon.

Sea crabs, or *grancevole*, are very flavorful. In season, they are a delicious introduction to a sampling of seafood. To follow: sardines (below, right), often served al saor—in a sweet-sour sauce. One must also try the tender and marrowy *castraure*, the small artichokes grown on San Erasmo and available only during the month of April (below, center).

The Da Romano trattoria is as familiar to the Burano fisherfolk as it is to artists and writers from the world over. It was founded by Romano Barbaro (1903–1964), who was considered one of the island's most important people. The traditional kitchen (above) opens onto the restaurant and the counter—a meeting-place for the island's fishermen.

In summer, the arbors of the Locanda Montin on Dorsoduro are pleasantly cool, as are Chez Franz's terraces along a canal in the Castello neighborhood. Many Venetians prefer the renowned Harry's Bar, or its "annex", Harry's Dolci—where the pastries are as rich as the passing scene on the Zattere.

On Giudecca, the homey Altanella is one of Venice's best fish
restaurants, with a terrace along
the rio del Ponte Longo. One of
the walls of Da Romano (left),
on Burano, is covered with paintings by all the artists who have
eaten here. In season, one orders
soft-shelled crabs (right).

where one ought to awaken in Venice, and that is at the Cipriani. Not just because it is Venice's most modern and luxurious hotel, located at the point of Giudecca, nor even because the city seems suddenly to have settled in the countryside that can be seen from certain rooms, the pleasure and vegetable gardens spreading out in front of the dome and graceful pinnacled turrets of the Palladian church of the Zitelle. Nor because the Cipriani offers what no other hotel in Venice can, and that is space. In its more-than-two-acre park, one can rest by the pool and orchestrate nature, beauty, and *far niente*. One has to wake up in the Cipriani and pass through its ocher and salmon-colored halls and sitting rooms hung with Fortuny fabrics to breakfast on one of the hotel's terraces in front of the lagoon. The Lido is a shadowy line in the distance. Rowers slip by on gondolas or *mascarete* in front of you. The water laps at your feet, a primal landscape in infinitely tender colors.

In my opinion, Venice is not a gastronomic capital—its spiritual and artistic nourishment are more impressive than its earthly food. Fine crystal, a brilliant damask tablecloth, a glimmering silver candelabrum, all these seem more precious to the city's inhabitants than a dish's extraordinary subtlety or the amount of oil in its sauce. Perhaps it is the mark of a great civilization to prefer the superfluous to the necessary to this degree. I wonder if the warmest, liveliest restaurants in Venice are not the simplest, those that aren't trying to achieve a standardized international menu, but are satisfied to provide an agreeable place for people to meet and to offer Venetian hospitality at its best: a simple polenta, seafood, fish fried or grilled, the succulent *risotto al nero di seppia*, or the famous *fegato alla veneziana*.

I would have liked to praise unreservedly the delicious *spaghetti ai carciofi* of a little restaurant near La Fenice, if the sight of the bill one evening had not made a connection for me between that written

The 1900-style decor of this small café in campo Santa Margherita, with its ancient copper coffee maker, is very unusual in Venice (top). Ice-cream shops are numerous in the Serenissima, in the squares and narrow streets. Each has its specialty, like gianduiotto—a chocolate and hazelnut confection (above). There is, however, only one Florian's in Venice (opposite, left top and bottom), just as there is only one way to serve a pastis: the water must be poured over the anise through crushed ice (opposite, right).

holdup and the name of the street on which it was taking place: degli Assassini! On the other hand, I remember gratefully the fresh pasta with braised black radishes (a vegetable from Treviso that the Venetians so expertly prepare a thousand different ways) that I enjoyed one evening after a wonderful performance of *Madama Butterfly* at La Fenice. It was one of the few restaurants open late, at the back of a little court on calle dei Fuseri. I was in a lyrical mood; the modest, slightly atonal harmony of the sweet *tagliatelle* and the faint bitterness of the radishes filled me with happiness.

The restaurants of Venice are sometimes tinged with a grace due as much to the perfection of light or the urgency or patience of my appetite as to the objective quality of dishes ordered on any particular day. Looking back, however, I can cite certain soft-shelled crabs (*moleche*, in Venetian dialect) that shed their shells and grow new ones around the end of October. I had them grilled, having discovered them at Corte Sconta, near the Arsenale. It is Hugo Pratt's neighborhood restaurant, when he takes a break from dreaming and drawing the adventures of his celebrated Corto Maltese. There was also a simple plate of pasta with mussels at a picturesque Murano restaurant where fishermen populate the bar; where the hedonistic gourmands prefer to sit at tables on the terrace amid the animation of via Baldassare Galuppi; and where those who like privacy choose the tables in the back between the bar and the kitchen, beneath paintings, posters, and photographs of the regulars.

But where did I treat myself one evening to a *braciola alla veneziana*, a breaded pork chop cooked with vinegar? Perhaps it was in the calm, bohemian intimacy of an artists' restaurant near San Trovaso, whose long, arbored garden provides a delightful place to linger on summer evenings. A table was always kept free for painters and writers, and Ezra Pound sometimes dined there, silent and enigmatic,

How is one to choose among Venice's wine bars, the bacari? Not far from the Pescheria, the rustic Do Mori, the city's oldest (above), offers a delectable assortment of snacks to accompany a glass of prosecco.

Another bacaro, the picturesque Mascaron, near Santa Maria Formosa (left; top, left), also prepares daily specials. Venetians enjoy the lunchtime bustle. They have long frequented as well the delightful Al Million (top, right), obviously named in honor of Marco Polo. The home of the illustrious traveler and his family is no longer standing, but it was said to have been here, behind the church of San Giovanni Crisostomo.

toward the end of his life. Or it may have been at the Mascaron, Santa Maria Formosa, with its wooden benches, rustic decor, and friendly, jostling lunchtime, when everyone crowds the bar to point out their own *antipasti*—herring and polenta, seafood, fritters, creamed cod salad—before the main course *du jour*.

The list of cafés in Venice is unchanging. On the same side as the Procuratie Vecchie the luxurious Quadri unfolds, its terrace a pleasant place to while away sunny mornings. On the side of the Procuratie Nuove is the ultrafamous, indispensable Florian, with its pretty tables beneath the arcade. The Florian wears its two and a half centuries well, and was loved by Goethe, Casanova, Chateaubriand, Lord Byron, and all those who are Venetian in their hearts and by adoption. The hot chocolate is as sublime as ever, creamy and dense enough to hold up the spoon. In the nineteenth century, the Quadri served as the rallying point for the officers of the Austrian occupation. The Florian, at the same time, with its small rooms sporting cherry-red banquettes, some of the rooms decorated with paintings under glass (among them, the famous *Chinaman*, so beloved of so many turn-of-the-century French writers like Henri de Régnier), became the headquarters of the Italian patriots. Nothing has changed since then. In February 1990, in one of the Florian's back rooms, I attended a meeting of angry young Venetians who were organizing their insurrection against the Venice world's fair, planned for the year 2000. They felt it had been imposed upon them by "foreigners"—industrialists from the Veneto, politicians from Rome—and with their dark looks, full beards, open shirts, and eloquent fervor they were the image of conspiring Risorgimento *carbonari*. In Venice, time sometimes stands still.

Blessedly neglected by tourists, the little wine bars are more intimate. They are called *bacari*, the etymology of the name reaching back to Bacchus. It is

Often missed by tourists, the Querini-Stampalia palace, both a library and a picture gallery, is a handsome example of the eighteenth-century style whose festive gaiety characterizes so many Venetian buildings. Note the pastel stuccowork of the receiving rooms en suite (above), the detail of a wood cherub in the reading room (below), and the splendid painted ceiling over a Murano chandelier (opposite).

pleasant to take a *prosecco frizzante* at the bar; the dry, slightly sparkling white wine goes straight to one's head. Or one of the little wines from the Valdobbiadene or the Colli Veronesi—the choice is great among the vineyards and varieties of northeastern Italy. The charming Al Milion has old wooden beams, and lace-edged shades on its hanging lamps. Just by the Rialto, at the back of an almost unfindable court, Al Milion makes it easy to imagine the now-vanished house of Marco Polo and his family. My favorite *bacari*, though, are still those that crowd around the *pescheria*. There is a small *cantina* where, in a dim and friendly atmosphere barely brightened by glints from the copper cauldrons hanging from the ceiling, the regulars come and go, the wholesalers, customers, and sellers of the Rialto market. A glass at the bar, off to work, then back again with other friends for another *ombra*, the little glass of wine that is believed to be named for the little movable stalls that once moved around Saint Mark's Square in order to follow the campanile's shadow—*ombra*—thus keeping the bottles cool. It is a good idea when at the bar, to have a snack between drinks—shrimp fritters, salmon sandwiches, or some fried *calamari*—to keep one's feet on Venice's relatively solid ground.

The most irresistible intoxication, however, is the past. The past has neither benumbed nor paralyzed the city, but rather spread to keep pace with it today. Like a scratched record on which the needle always skips back to the same groove, Venice's decors are stuck, so to speak, in the late eighteenth century. Against this same background music the generations have followed each other, the wavelets of progress have lapsed, new ways of working, thinking, trading, loving, dreaming, and being happy have been invented. The palazzi on the Grand Canal are by no means all patrician residences proudly locked into their glory days. Many have been turned into showrooms for Venice's most prestigious textile or glass-

makers, offices, or centers of learning.

Near the Rialto is the Fondaco dei Tedeschi, the stunning, monumental central post office of Venice, its great court today covered by three upstairs galleries. It is one of Venice's most unlikely secret places. Mailing a letter or sending a telegram is no longer a routine errand but an adventure, an historical, aesthetic exhilaration amid the buzzing voices that echo from one wall to another. Or wander about the conservatory of music at the palazzo Pisani, near the Accademia bridge. Don't be shy about climbing the stairs, or entering the breathtaking, *settecento* grand drawing room that resonates with the tones of a singer vocalizing, a trumpet player practicing scales, or an invisible pianist rippling from one octave to the next. No one will stop you, or dream of asking what you're doing there.

After all, it follows the logic of time, custom, and fortunes that the oldest Venetian families would often have had to give way to the new economic forces or seizures by state or local government. Thus the palazzo Labia became the offices of the R.A.I., the palazzo Grassi was bought by Fiat and restored (by Gae Aulenti and Antonio Foscari) so as to house great, prestigious exhibitions. Ca' Rezzonico, once owned by the poet Robert Browning, is now a charming museum dedicated to the eighteenth century. There, the exuberant ceilings painted by Tiepolo and

The library of the Fondazione Cini in San Giorgio Maggiore (left); the rooms of the Biblioteca Marciana, built by Sansovino on the piazzetta (below); and the baroque eighteenth-century drawing room in the Ca' Rezzonico (right) are all treasures of an often-unexplored Venice.

The Ca' Zenobio (opposite), to-day the seat of the Armenian College, is unquestionably the finest example of an eighteenth-century Venetian palace. Its ball-room, with its profuse and whirl-ing stuccowork, is one of the most lavish in Venice. There are other secret places for the Serenissima's devotées. Above the baroque church of Santa Maria della Fava in the library of the Redemptorist Fathers, one may attend an organ concert (left). The impressive Pisani palace to-day houses the conservatory of music, a lyrical setting indeed for learning the bassoon (right).

231

The gran teatro *La Fenice*, one of the world's most beautiful and famous opera houses, is perfectly suited to Rossini, Donizetti, and the overwhelming delights of bel canto. Although the backrest of the armchair in the box of honor sports the doge's hat as a decorative emblem, the theater, designed by Selva, was finished in 1792, subsequent to the Most Serene Republic's grander days. (Right) A detail of the painted, recently restored *rido storico*.

La Fenice's grand box reveals extravagant arabesques, the beautiful colored drape of the scene curtain, and a foyer with painted ceilings. Moviegoers will perhaps be reminded of the beginning of Visconti's *Senso*, which borrowed from La Fenice's decor to raise the curtain on the 1866 uprising of Venetian patriots against the Austrian occupation.

Longhi harmonize in a bygone past.

Few are the visitors to the palazzo Querini Stampalia, which stands in a charming *campo* of few meters from Santa Maria Formosa. The picture collection on the third floor displays in particular a series of eighteenth-century paintings that describe daily life in Venice and all its neighborhoods in naive and pungent detail. And one cannot ignore the illustrious Biblioteca Marciana, by Sansovino, on the *piazzetta* facing the Doges' Palace. Its grand drawing room, with its paintings by Veronese, Titian, and Andrea Schiavone, is without a doubt the most majestic and magnificent one I know in Venice, and the one that best conveys the city's splendor, elegance, and richness. The room is not open to the public every day,

This casinò, *or ridotto,* near *the Ponte dei Baratteri, was one of the gaming and pleasure clubs of Venetian noblemen. It is said to have belonged to Elena Priuli, wife of the attorney Federico Venier. The attractive tile floor, stuccowork, and graceful harmony of its rooms all testify to the happy, frivolous last days of the Republic of Venice at the end of the eighteenth century.*

but the caretaker can be persuaded to give a tour. I know few Venetians who are reluctant to do strangers the honor of Venice, their Venice. I remember the Ca' Zenobio, not far from the Carmini, which is today the home of an Armenian College. I wanted to visit its great Baroque drawing room and its Tiepolesque frescoes, so I telephoned to make an appointment. Father Raphael Andonian, the institution's director, received me with charming courtesy, and we had an impromptu two-hour discussion on the problem of the dual nature of Christ, the Nicene Council of 325, and the differences between the Armenian Catholic Church and the Armenian Apostolic Church, before he showed us all the nooks, crannies, and treasures of the Ca' Zenobio, including its vast garden and small, Palladian-style library.

Venice lies in such encounters and surprises—on Sundays at San Giorgio Maggiore, its religious fervor unmasked, when the Benedictines sing the Gregorian mass, and in the modest church of Santa Maria della Fava, which resounds with the wonderful, almost pastoral tone of a merry little Baroque organ.

Of course, lyrical Venice still meets at La Fenice, its pure and elegant Neoclassical portico reaching out toward the church of San Fantin. The hall was rebuilt following a fire in 1837 (how apt the name fenice— "phoenix"), and the acoustics are some of the most marvellous anywhere. The elegant tones of old gold and pale blue vibrate as if anticipating bel canto. I think gratefully of Daniele Paolin, the Fenice's scenographer and technical director. One January morning he took me backstage into the attics, the workshops, and the thousand places of that warren. I have also found the gallant, frivolous Venice, the Venice of the last years of the Republic, in the intimacy of a delightful ridotto, or casino (one of the small, private rooms reserved for gaming and other pleasures owned by Venetian nobles) like that of the Procuratessa Venier, near the Ponte dei Baratteri, on the Mercerie.

In the northern part of the city, in the Cannaregio neighborhood, the fifteenth-century Giovanelli palace today houses Venice's casa d'asta, or auction house. The palm trees around the courtyard's beautiful Gothic well add an exotic element, as do the curious stone elephants that appear to stand guard in the entrance hall. The building was considerably reworked in the nineteenth century by the architect Meduna, who designed the great octagonal neo-Gothic staircase beneath an elegant glass roof.

It is three little rooms bright with stuccowork ceilings and pink walls, and has a secret door, an area out of sight so the musicians who played could not identify any of the guests. It also has a *cabochon* that one pulls out of the floor to spy the visitors knocking on the outside door, under the portico. Suddenly, Giacomo Casanova's wildest adventures flood one's memory and senses. Today, the Venier casino houses the Alliance Française. You will not be turned away.

One more time: the Venetian past and culture are not bogged down by dusty, inert veneration. On the contrary, they surface in everyday life and bring to it the rendezvous that Venice proposes to those who love it. One has only to wander behind the scenes, *dietro le quinte*, as the Italians say. Take, for example, Venice's auction rooms, its *casa d'asta*, in palazzo Giovanelli. There, in Cannaregio, in a wonderful Gothic edifice (somewhat less wonderfully restored at the end of the nineteenth century, this time with an octagonal, neo-Gothic grand staircase), in great, handsome drawing rooms with frescoes and stuccowork in a very late eighteenth-century style, are piled the furniture, chairs, and paintings that will be bid on. On Giudecca, left of the church of the Redentore, Serafin's junk shop is an extravagant labyrinth, its alleys and paths sometimes covered, sometimes out in the open. One finds amassed there what Serafin has bought from everybody for more than thirty years: typewriters that no longer type, ventilators that no longer ventilate, night tables sunk in eternal sleep, carved panels from centuries-old gondolas, faience plates with the names of Venice's luxury hotels, and so on. Serafin has everything imaginable—and unimaginable. What the city remembers, forgets, rejects, and scorns all washes up at his place. You must know how to rummage there. Time has stopped in this Ali Baba's cave, where Venice keeps telling us what we have already guessed: that it is a magical city. The only truly, totally, uniquely magical city in the world.

The extravagant disarray of Serafin's secondhand shop on Giudecca recalls an attic—a collection of relics, unsold goods, antique treasures, battered furniture, plaster busts, and madonnas abandoned by the faithful. The atmosphere of this Ali Baba's cave is the oppressive, dusty, exhilarating scent of bygone days. An antique dealer like Zancope of San Maurizio has, of course, much more prestige. On display in his store are these two beautiful sixteenth-century glass reliquaries (right).

Is Venice a city of the past? Perhaps, but it is also a city where the past continually surfaces into the present. Venice is heaven for lovers of secondhand shops. Exploring shops on the Grand Canal or down an obscure calle, they will find—as at this antique dealer's on the Grand Canal near the Ca' Rezzonico—chairs, banners, trumpets, swords, old color-prints, etchings, and fragments of gondolas. On these treasure hunts they might find what they wish, or what they dream of, or even what they've never imagined.

(Following page) Detail of a door knocker bearing a lion, the timeless emblem of Venice.

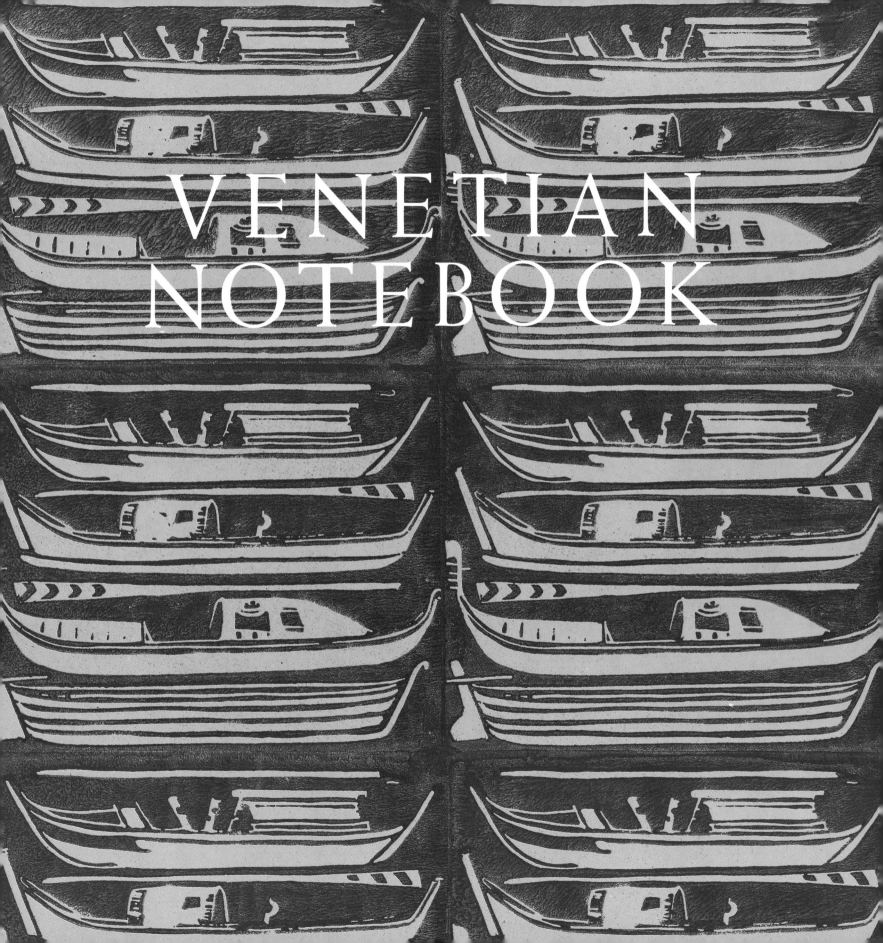

VENETIAN
NOTEBOOK

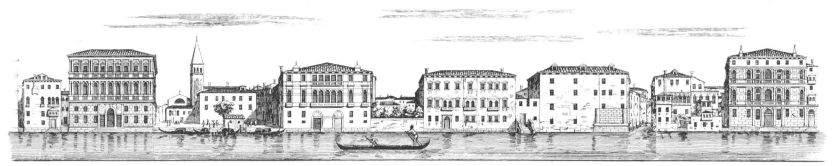

These addresses were provided by those gracious Venetians who opened their doors to the authors. Some are very well known, others less so. You will find many of the addresses of the artisans, hotels, and bars that are mentioned in the text or shown in the photographs, with page references. We have limited our selection of museums to those that were once private homes and have retained their decor and charm. The notebook is organized by neighborhoods. Unfortunately, you have to go to San Marco, the area most frequented by tourists, to shop, but you might want to stay in Dorsoduro, a neighborhood that numbers a great many charming little pensioni. You can dine away from the crowds in San Polo, Castello, or Cannaregio.

Addresses in Venice are comprised of the name of the area and the house number, but this information never tells you where the place is located, so one usually has to look in several guidebooks. We have therefore indicated, before the house number, the street, square, or quay that is easiest to find (see map pp. 246–47). The hours and days when places close vary, so we have included telephone numbers. Venice is a very expensive city, so consider the wine bars, rather than restaurants, for light meals. And be aware that the price of coffee in piazza San Marco goes up the moment the musicians start to play.

SAN MARCO

HOTELS

Flora
Calle Largo XXII Marzo
Tel. 520 58 44
Located in the heart of the tourist quarter, this hotel has a secret garden.

La Fenice et des Artistes
Campiello della Fenice 1936
Tel. 523 23 33
A meeting place for singers and directors from the opera.

Gritti
See p. 212
Campo S. Maria del Giglio 2467
Tel. 79 46 11
Known for its terrace restaurant on the Grand Canal and for its annex, the *Palazzo del Giglio*, rents apartments for a few days or a few months.

RESTAURANTS

Da Raffaele
Fa delle Ostreghe 2347
Tel. 523 23 17
Despite the gondoliers who wait for clients in front of the tables by the canal, this good restaurant is also frequented by Venetians.

Harry's Bar
Calle Vallaresso 1323
Tel. 523 67 97
A table on the ground floor is the best place to experience this legendary bar.

Da Ivo
Ramo dei Fuseri 1809
Tel. 520 58 59
A good place to sample white truffles in season.

Alla Colomba
Piscina di Frezzeria 1665
Tel. 522 11 75
Handsome modern decor and good cooking. Elegant. Large terrace.

Da Arturo
Calle degli Assassini 3656
Tel. 528 69 74
Tiny. Good wines.

CAFÉS

Florian
See p. 223
Piazza San Marco 56–59
Tel. 528 53 38
The chocolates and cocktails are famous. A delightful place to meet in piazza San Marco.

Quadri
Piazza San Marco 120
Tel. 522 21 05
For outdoor breakfasts. A very elegant restaurant recently opened on the second floor.

Paolin
Campo Santo Stefano 2962/A
Tel. 522 55 76
A well-placed bar for a *spritz* (an *aperitivo* consisting of *prosecco* and bitters) or an ice cream.

WINE BARS

Vino vino
Calle della Veste 2007/A
Tel. 522 41 21
A modern wine bar where musicians from La Fenice congregate.

Al Bacereto
San Samuele 3447
Tel. 528 93 36
Another very lively place for simple, tasty cooking.

PASTRY SHOPS

Marchini
Ponte San Maurizio 2769
Tel. 522 91 09
The city's best cakes. Their *morellina*, an unforgettable chocolate cake, must be ordered two days in advance.

Rosa Salva
Campo San Luca
or Calle Fiubera Tel. 522 53 85
Delicious cakes and a selection of sandwiches.

BREADS AND COOKIES

Panificio Colussi
Calle della Mandole 3726
Tel. 522 46 28

Il Fornaio
Salizada San Luca 4579
Tel. 522 26 59
A beautiful bakery with a good selection of breads and pâtés.

FABRICS

Venetia Studium
Campo San Fantin 1997
Tel. 523 69 53
Modern copies of Fortuny fabrics and lamps.

Lorenzo Rubelli
Campo San Gallo 1089
Tel. 523 61 10
Very beautiful silk damasks and hand-woven velvets. Furnishing fabrics can also be found at the palazzo Corner Spinelli on the Grand Canal.

V. Troïs
See p. 200
Campo San Maurizio 2660
Tel. 522 29 05
The only outlet for Fortuny fabrics. Your choice of cotton-and-gold damasks, after the models Fortuny created in silk velvet.

Gaggio
Campo Santo Stefano 3451
Tel. 522 85 74
Beautiful hand-painted fabrics and clothes.

PAPER

Legatoria Piazzesi
See pp. 204–205
Santa Maria del Giglio 2511/C
Tel. 522 12 02
The oldest shop selling hand-printed papers. They are bound in the shop into little notebooks, diaries, etc. Also not to be missed, the characters of the commedia dell'arte in hand-painted papier-mâché.

Alberto Valese—Ebrû
Calle della Fenice 1920
Salizada San Samuele 3135
Tel. 528 63 02 or 520 09 21
This marbled-paper maker transfers his designs to crêpe de Chine scarves.

GLASS

Venini
Piazzetta dei Leoncini 314
Tel. 522 40 45
A great glassmaking firm

L'Isola
Campo San Moisè 1468
Tel. 523 19 73
Discover the modern creations of Carlo Moretti.

Battiston
Calle Vallaresso 1320

Tel. 523 05 09
A good choice of works by well-known glassmakers.

Rigattieri
Calle della Mandola 3532
Tel. 523 1081
A wide choice of fine pieces from famous glassmakers: Seguso, Barovier e Toso, Venini, among others, located in a large shop between campo San Stefano and campo Sant' Angelo.

Archimede Seguso
Piazza San Marco 143
Tel. 522 6230
Explore the shop of the doyen of master glassmakers.

Jesurum
See p. 202
Ponte della Canonica 4310
Tel. 520 61 77
Located in the stunning surroundings of a thirteenth-century church. Antique linens and sheets, tablecloths, and curtains are embroidered to order.

JEWELRY

Nardi
Piazza San Marco 69
Tel. 523 21 50
The designer of among many other pieces, a famous clip portraying a Moor.

Missiaglia
Piazza Sa Marco 125
Tel. 522 44 64
Purveyor to the great families since 1836.

Attilio Codognato
Calle del Ascension 1295
Tel. 522 50 42
A very pretty shop that sells antique jewelry, just behind piazza San Marco.

BRONZE

Valese—Founder
See pp. 182, 188–89
Calle Fiubera
Tel. 522 72 82
Mario Valese's designs are sold in this shop: door knockers, doorknobs, gondola ornaments, lanterns, and other items, in bronze, copper, pewter, and wrought iron.

FRAMES

El Dorador
Campo Manin 4231
Tel. 528 73 16
Alfredo Barutti restores and sells gilt-wood furniture and frames.

BOOKS

Giocondo Cassini
Via XXII Marzo 2424
Tel. 523 18 15
Antique books and etchings.

Libreria Emiliana
Calle Goldoni 4487
Tel. 522 07 93
A vast selection of books on Venice in several languages.

Fantoni Libri
San Luca 4119
Tel. 522 07 00
A vast selection of art and illustrated books.

Libreria Editrice Filippi
Calle della Bissa 5458
Tel. 523 69 16
The widest selection of works on Venetian life—unfortunately, all in Italian—from this very talented publisher and bookseller.

Libreria Internazionale Sangiorgio
Calle Larga XXII Marzo 2087
Tel. 523 84 51
A good selection of books, guidebooks, and maps.

Libreria Goldoni
Calle dei Fabbri 4742
Tel. 522 23 84
A very good all-purpose bookstore, which offers, among other things, a drawing, in nine long plates, of all the houses on the Grand Canal—a facsimile edition of an 1828 work that may be seen at the Biblioteca Marciana.

MUSEUMS

Palazzo Grassi
Campo San Samuele 3231
Tel. 523 78 86 or 532 16 80
Tourists crowd its major exhibitions, but the pink-*marmorino*-walled cafeteria is calm and overlooks the Grand Canal. It is owned by the same people who own Harry's Bar.

Museo Fortuny
At the end of rio terrà della Mandola 3780
Tel. 520 09 95
Fortuny's home until his death in 1949. All his creations are displayed here.

Biblioteca Marciana
See p. 228
Piazzetta San Marco
Tel. 520 87 88
Admire the rooms of this venerable library, or consult one of its 750,000 volumes.

Casino Venier
See pp. 2, 234–35
Ponte dei Bareteri 4939
Tel. 522 70 79

An exquisite frame for occasional exhibits.

PRIVATE TOURS

Venezia per voi
San Marco 3316
Tel. 522 24 33
Founders Lucia Zavagli Ricciardelli and Yaya Masutti organize exceptional events for tourists visiting Venice: a ball or a meal in a palace, visits to artists' studios, cooking lessons, private concerts.

POST OFFICE

In the former Fondaco dei tedeschi, a sixteenth-century warehouse.

MUSIC

La Fenice
See pp. 232–33
Campo San Fantin 30124
Tel. 78 65 11
Concerts and opera. The season runs from January to May.

Santa Maria della Fava
See p. 231
Campo Fava
Organ concerts.

Palazzo Pisani
See p. 231
Campiello Pisani 2810
Tel. 522 56 04
The interior courts and the rooms of this former palace—now academy of music—are a magnificent setting. *Don't Look Now*, based on a novel by Daphne du Maurier, was shot here.

TRICORNS

Amalia Marzato
See p. 200
Calle del Lovo 4813
Tel. 522 64 54
For Carnival.

PALACES FOR RENT

Palazzetto Pisani
Santo Stefano 2814
Tel. 528 53 43
This palace on the Grand Canal belongs to the Contessa Ferri, a direct descendant of the dogal Pisani family. Receptions, grand dinners, and concerts may be held there, while the *piano nobile* and ground floor are available as service apartments.

ANTIQUES

Paolo Emanuele Zancope
See p. 238
Campo San Maurizio
Tel. 523 45 67
Specializes in antique glassware.

DORSODURO

HOTELS

Pensione Accademia
Fondamenta Bollani 1058
Tel. 523 78 46
Located between two gardens on the rio di San Trovaso, this is one of the most delightful small pensioni. Make reservations well in advance.

Hotel American
San Vio 628
Tel. 520 47 33
A small hotel, well situated on the rio San Vio.

Pensione Seguso
Zattere 779
Tel. 522 23 40
Decorated with antique furniture. The third-floor room with balconies overlooking the intersection of two canals is the best, but has no bathroom.

Pensione la Calcina
Zattere 780
Tel. 520 64 66
Watch the cruise ships glide up the Giudecca canal.

Hotel Pausania
Fondamenta Gherardini 2824
Tel. 522 20 83
A former palace with a very pretty traditional courtyard, located near San Barnaba.

RESTAURANTS

La Furatola
Calle Lunga San Barnaba 2870
Tel. 520 85 94
A simple restaurant, well-liked by the locals.

Montin
See p. 220
Fondamenta Eremite 1147
Tel. 522 71 51
Large, cheerful rooms and a very large garden. Traditional Venetian cuisine.

Riviera
Zattere 1473
Tel. 522 76 21
Run by an ex-chef at Harry's Bar. A very good little restaurant with sunny tables by the Giudecca canal.

Ai Cugnai
San Vio 857
Tel. 528 92 38
A good, simple little trattoria.

Da Gianni
Zattere 918
Tel. 523 72 10
A good pizzeria. A large, sunny terrace.

Codroma
Ponte del Soccorso 2540

Tel. 70 41 61
Old-style decor in this students' bistro.

CAFÉS

Linea d'ombra
Zattere 19
Tel. 528 52 59
A large terrace near the Salute. Piano bar in the evening.

Il Caffè
See p. 222
Campo Santa Margherita 2963
Tel. 528 79 98
A tiny café with turn-of-the-century decor and a splendid copper coffeemaker.

Cucciolo
Zattere 782
Tel. 528 96 41
The best coffee in Venice. Sandwiches and pizzas.

De Maravegie
Calle de la Toletta 1185
Tel. 523 57 68
For a delicious breakfast before visiting the Accademia. Opens very early. *Frullati* and *spremute*: as in many bars in the city, there is a great selection of freshly squeezed juices and fruit whips served here.

PASTRY

Vio
Calle de la Toletta 1192
Tel. 522 74 51
A good selection of cakes. A branch of Marchini (*see* SAN MARCO).

PASTA

Pastificio Battiston
Calle San Pantalon 3750
Tel. 520 65 58

A wide selection of fresh pasta.

ICE CREAM

Causin
Campo Santa Margherita 2996
Tel. 523 60 91
One of the best ice-cream shops in the city. Its specialty is *gelato sublime*.

Gelateria Nico
Zattere 922
Tel. 522 52 93
A large, sunny terrace for sampling their specialty, *Gianduiotto*.

MARKET

On campo Santa Margherita every day except Sunday and Monday.

FABRICS

Arianna di Venezia
Dorsoduro 2793
Tel. 522 15 35
At the Ca' Rezzonico vaporetto stop, a pretty shop with old-fashioned raised velvets and tricorns.

ANTIQUES

Giorgio Crosara
See p. 239
Pontile Ca' Rezzonico 2793/A
Restored antique furniture. A very pretty shop opening onto the canal.

MUSEUMS

Collezione Peggy Guggenheim
San Gregorio 701
Tel. 520 62 88
Peggy Guggenheim lived in this house until her death. Her collection is exhibited in all the

rooms of the palace. Pleasant garden.

Galleria di Palazzo Cini
San Vio 864
Tel. 521 07 55
A small, seventeenth-century palace with a fine collection and a beautiful dining room.

Palazzo Zenobio
See p. 230
Fondamenta del Soccorso 2596
Tel. 522 87 70
One of the most beautiful palaces in Venice, and presently the seat of the Armenian College. Visitors are graciously received and concerts are held here.

Ca' Rezzonico
See p. 228–229
Fondamenta Rezzonico at San Barnaba
Tel. 522 45 43
The museum of the seventeenth-century with a splendid chandelier in the grand drawing room and some fine pieces of furniture.

PALACE RECEPTIONS

Palazzetto da Schio
Fondamenta Soranzo 316/B
Tel. 523 79 37
This small palace near the Salute belongs to the family of the conti da Schio. Their descendants will show you around the palace and offer you an *ombra* in the charming garden.

BOATS

Squero San Trovaso
Campo San Trovaso 10977
Tel. 522 91 46

Venice's most photographed *squero*. Gondolas are built or repaired under Ettore Nardo's management.

Società Bucintoro
See p. 31
Fondamenta de la Salute 15
Tel. 522 20 54
One of the best spots in Venice to watch the *Vogalonga*. There are boats to row Venetian- or English-style. They have ten-lesson courses for foreigners.

MODERN ART

Roberto Ferruzzi
Fondamenta Ca' Venier 710
Tel. 520 59 96
Ferruzzi, a painter, has his own gallery. As you stroll through Dorsoduro, you'll be able to tell which house is his by the fresco he has painted on the wall.

MASKS

Mondonovo
Ponte dei Pugni 3063
Tel. 528 73 44
The only mask shop we recommend. There are many others—they are as plentiful as pigeons. This one makes masks that are replicas of the old models, but also fills your most fanciful orders.

PAPUZZE

Gianni Dittura
Calle Nova Sant' Agnese
Tel. 523 11 63
A stone's throw from the Accademia, the shop offers a wide selection of *papuzze*—the gondoliers' velvet slippers—in every color.

SCULPTURE

Antonio Luccarda
See pp. 152–53
San Lio Corte del Sabbion 478
Tel. 522 25 98
You can have a bronze minibust
made of yourself, or a medal.

SAN POLO

RESTAURANTS

Poste Vecie
Pescheria 1608
Tel. 72 18 22
A very good fish restaurant.

Da Fiore
Calle del Scaleter 2202
Tel. 72 13 08
One of the best fish restaurants
on campo San Polo, serving a
perfect risotto and a memora-
ble dessert, *mascarpone e amaretti*.

Caffè Orientale
Rio Marin-Ponte della Latte
Tel. 71 98 04
An Art Deco interior and good
cooking—a delight on a small
terrace that opens onto the
canal.

WINE BARS

Do Mori
See p. 224
Calle dei Do Mori 429
Tel. 522 54 01
Near the Rialto bridge, this is
one of the best *bacari*, especially for stopping in after a
walk to the market. If you
are planning to have lunch,
be aware that it closes at
1:00 p.m.

Do Spade
Calle de le Do Spade
Tel. 521 05 74
This street is an extension of
Calle dei Do Mori, making this
bar your next stop—the selec-
tion at the counter is also
interesting.

CHEESE

Sbrissa
Rialto 88–90
Tel. 52 42 10
A wide selection of cheeses
from the Veneto.

LACE

Cenerentola
Calle dei Saoneri 2721
Tel. 523 20 06
A fine selection of antique laces
and a very charming welcome.

ANTIQUES

Michele Cicogna
See p. 206
Campo San Toma 2867
Tel. 522 76 78
This furniture restorer displays
in his shop window antique fur-
niture and objects for sale.

TAPESTRY MAKER

Pasinetti
See pp. 198–99
Campiello Ca' Bernardi 1321
Tel. 522 32 65
Restorers of antique fabrics.
Restores and makes tapestries;
also makes costumes for
Carnival.

GOLDSMITH

Sfriso
See pp. 186–87
Campo San Toma 2849
Tel. 522 35 58

Silver ewers, basins, candle-
sticks, and silverware. Official
gifts often come from this shop
over which the Sfriso brothers
preside.

SMALL MUSEUMS

Casa Goldoni
See p. 4–5, 70
Calle dei Nombili 2794
Tel. 523 63 53
The house in which Goldoni
was born. The interior court-
yard is particularly interesting.

BOOKBINDER

Ex Libris
See p. 184, 205
Ponte della Madonnetta 1462
Tel. 522 40 04
Binding, restoration of antique
books, hand-printed paper, and
objects covered in endpaper.

MARKET

See pp 56–57
Between campo San Giacomo
di Rialto and campo della
Pescheria. Every day except
Sunday and Monday.

SANTA CROCE

HOTEL

Al Sole
Santa Croce 136
Tel. 523 21 44
A recently restored palace not
far from the train station and
the Papadopoli gardens.

PASTRY

**Boutique del Dolce—
Gilda Vio**
Rio Marin 890
Tel. 71 85 23

If you follow the rio Marin you
will see the kitchen, in the
window of which are prepared
all the cakes sold in the shop
across the canal.

FABRICS

Luigi Bevilacqua
See pp. 196–97
Campo San Giovanni
Decollato
Tel. 72 13 84
Silk velvets and hand-woven
brocades, the most sumptuous
Venice has to offer.

MUSEUMS

Palazzo Mocenigo
San Stae 1992
Behind the church of San Stae,
this palazzo is a research center for the history of fabrics
and costume. The library is
open to the public. One may
visit the Mocenigo apartment,
which is decorated with
eighteenth-century frescoes
and furniture, on Saturdays
from 8:30 a.m. to 1:30 p.m.

CANNAREGIO

HOTELS

Madonna dell' Orto
Fondamenta Madonna dell'
Orto 3499
A charming hotel with a fine
garden.

RESTAURANTS

Fiascheteria Toscana
Salizada San Giovanni
Crisostomo
Tel. 528 52 81
Despite its name, it serves
good Venetian specialties, in-

cluding a *risotto de go*.

Osteria al Bacco
Fa delle Cappuccine 3054
Tel. 71 74 93
A very good restaurant occupy-
ing a former wine seller's shop.

All' Antica Mola
Fa degli Ormesini 2800
Tel. 71 74 92
A small trattoria near the *ghetto*
with simple fare.

WINE BARS

Osteria al Milion
See p. 225
Corte prima del Milion
Tel. 522 93 02
A good place to sample *moleche*
(soft-shell crabs) when in sea-
son, or a wide selection of
cicchetti.

Ca' d'Oro
Calle del Pistor 3912
Tel. 528 53 24
Behind the Ca' d'Or, this *bacaro*
is decorated with antique
decor, a style Venetians call
alla Vedova.

PASTA

Pastificio G. Rizzo
San Giovanni Crisostomo 5778
or San Leonardo 1593
Tel. 522 28 24 or 71 74 94
A dizzying selection of pasta.
Also the only source in Venice
of bitter strawberry-tree honey
(*miele amaro di corbezzolo*).

ANTIQUES

Palazzo Giovanelli
See pp. 236–37
Strada Nova 2292
Tel. 72 18 11
The city's auction hall, in an

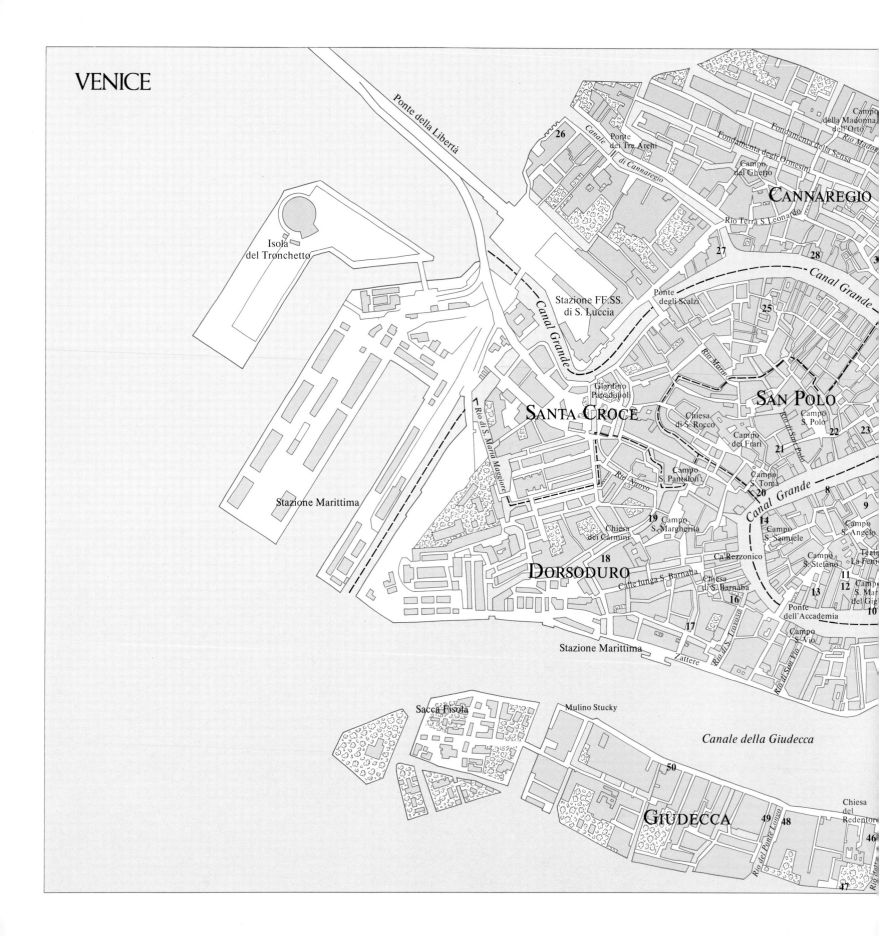

VENICE

CANNAREGIO

Campo della Madonna dell'Orto

Fondamenta della Sensa

Fondamenta degli Ormesini

Campo del Ghetto

26

Canale di Cannaregio

Ponte dei Tre Archi

Rio Terra S. Leonardo

Rio Mador

Ponte della Libertà

Isola del Tronchetto

Stazione FF.SS. di S. Luccia

Ponte degli Scalzi

27   28

Canal Grande

25

Canal Grande

Rio Marin

Giardino Papadopoli

SANTA CROCE

1   Rio di S. Maria Maggiore

Chiesa di S. Rocco

SAN POLO

Campo S. Polo

22   23

Campo dei Frari

21

Rio di San Polo

Rio Novo

Campo S. Pantalon

Campo S. Toma

20

Campo S. Stin

14

Canal Grande

8

9

Campo S. Samuele

Campo S. Angelo

19   Campo S. Margherita

Chiesa dei Carmini

Ca'Rezzonico

Campo S. Stefano

Teatro La Feni

18

DORSODURO

Calle lunga S. Barnaba

Chiesa di S. Barnaba

16

13

11

Campo S. Mar del Gig

12

10

17

Rio di S. Trovaso

Ponte dell'Accademia

Campo S. Vio

Stazione Marittima

Stazione Marittima

Zattere

Rio di Sant'Eufemia

Sacca Fisola

Mulino Stucky

Canale della Giudecca

50

49   48

Chiesa del Redentor

GIUDECCA

Rio del Ponte Lungo

46

47

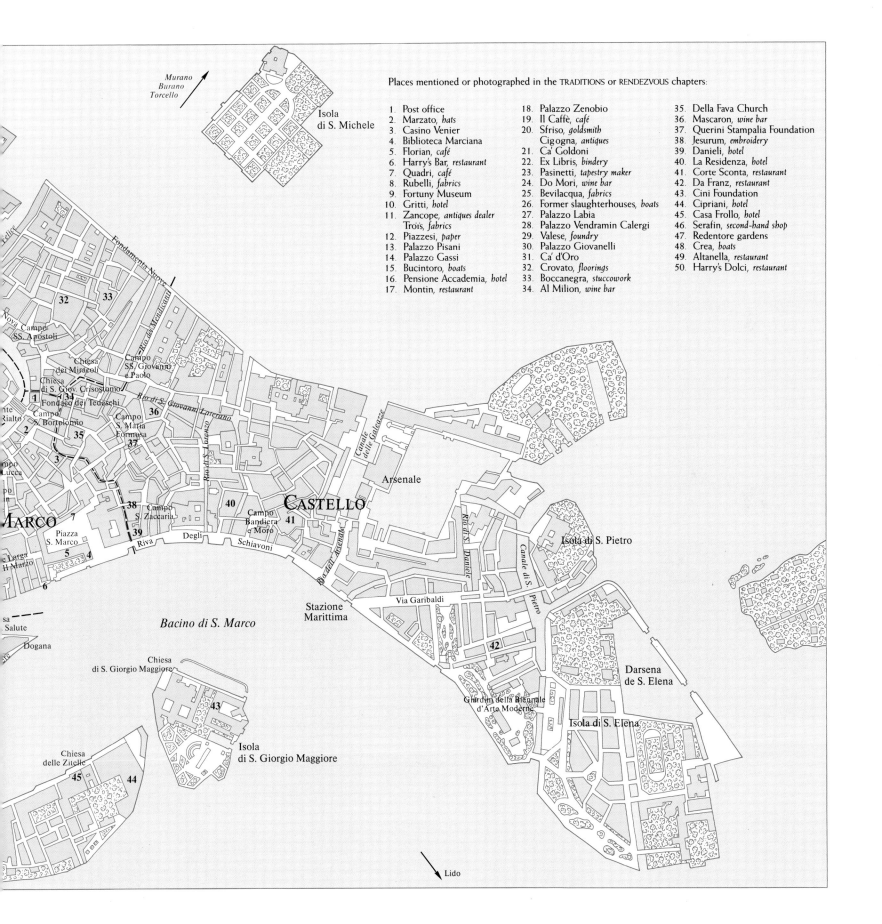

Murano
Burano
Torcello

Isola
di S. Michele

Places mentioned or photographed in the TRADITIONS or RENDEZVOUS chapters:

1. Post office
2. Marzato, *hats*
3. Casino Venier
4. Biblioteca Marciana
5. Florian, *café*
6. Harry's Bar, *restaurant*
7. Quadri, *café*
8. Rubelli, *fabrics*
9. Fortuny Museum
10. Gritti, *hotel*
11. Zancope, *antiques dealer*
    Trois, *fabrics*
12. Piazzesi, *paper*
13. Palazzo Pisani
14. Palazzo Gassi
15. Bucintoro, *boats*
16. Pensione Accademia, *hotel*
17. Montin, *restaurant*

18. Palazzo Zenobio
19. Il Caffè, *café*
20. Sfriso, *goldsmith*
    Cigogna, *antiques*
21. Ca' Goldoni
22. Ex Libris, *bindery*
23. Pasinetti, *tapestry maker*
24. Do Mori, *wine bar*
25. Bevilacqua, *fabrics*
26. Former slaughterhouses, *boats*
27. Palazzo Labia
28. Palazzo Vendramin Calergi
29. Valese, *foundry*
30. Palazzo Giovanelli
31. Ca' d'Oro
32. Crovato, *floorings*
33. Boccanegra, *stuccowork*
34. Al Milion, *wine bar*

35. Della Fava Church
36. Mascaron, *wine bar*
37. Querini Stampalia Foundation
38. Jesurum, *embroidery*
39. Danieli, *hotel*
40. La Residenza, *hotel*
41. Corte Sconta, *restaurant*
42. Da Franz, *restaurant*
43. Cini Foundation
44. Cipriani, *hotel*
45. Casa Frollo, *hotel*
46. Serafin, *second-hand shop*
47. Redentore gardens
48. Crea, *boats*
49. Altanella, *restaurant*
50. Harry's Dolci, *restaurant*

Fondamenta Nuove

Rio dei Mendicanti

Chiesa
dei Miracoli

Campo
SS. Giovanni
e Paolo

Nova Campo
SS. Apostoli

Chiesa
di S. Giov. Crisostomo

Fondaco dei Tedeschi

Campo
S. Bortolomio

Campo
S. Maria
Formosa

Rio di S. Giovanni Laterano

Ponte
Rialto

Campo
Lucca

Rio S. Lorenzo

Arsenale

CASTELLO

Campo
S. Zaccaria

Campo
Bandiera
e Moro

Canale delle Galeazze

Rio di S. Daniele

Isola di S. Pietro

MARCO

Piazza
S. Marco

Riva   Degli   Schiavoni

Canale di S. Pietro

Bacino di S. Marco

Stazione
Marittima

Via Garibaldi

Darsena
de S. Elena

Chiesa
di S. Giorgio Maggiore

Dogana

Salute

Giardini della Biennale
d'Arte Moderna

Isola di S. Elena

Chiesa
delle Zitelle

Isola
di S. Giorgio Maggiore

Lido

astonishing patrician home belonging to the antiques dealer Franco Semenzato.

BRONZES

Valese Fonditore
See pp. 182, 188–89
Fondamenta Madonna dell'
Orto 3535
Tel. 72 02 34
Mario Valese welcomes tourists, but only by appointment, because the foundry doesn't operate every day.

STUCCOWORK

Giuseppe Boccanegra
See p. 185
Calle San Antonio 4738
Tel. 522 05 63
Restorers of stuccowork. Make an appointment by calling the San Marco office at the above telephone number.

MUSEUM

Palazzo Labia
Campo San Geremia
Tel. 71 66 66 or 78 11 11
Call for an appointment to see the extraordinary Tiepolo drawing room in the R.A.I. building.

PLACES TO MARRY

Santa Maria dei Miracoli
Campo dei Miracoli
Behind campo Santa Maria Nuova and not far from campo San Giovanni e Paolo, this is undoubtedly the prettiest church in Venice in which to be married.

BOATS

Canottiere Vio

Rio Madonna dell' Orto 3541
Tel. 72 10 22
Japanese and Californian clients are especially devoted to this boat yard which builds *motoscafo* of the finest woods.

**Remiera Canottieri
Cannaregio**
See pp. 30–31
Fondamenta San Giobbe 732
Tel. 72 05 39
A rowing club in a Neoclassic setting, formerly the city slaughterhouses.

FLOORING

**Ditta Crovato Antonio di
Crovato Roberto**
See pp. 206–207
Calle dei Biri 5392/A
Tel. 523 23 59
Makers of authentic Venetian terrazzo flooring. Antonio Crovato, who has restored Venice's most beautiful palaces, has published an entire book on the subject of terrazzo.

CASTELLO

HOTELS

Pensione del Bucintoro
Riva San Biagio 2134
Tel. 522 32 40
A tranquil, simple little pensione. All the rooms have views over Saint Mark's Basin.

La Residenza
Campo Bandiera e Moro 3608
Tel. 528 53 15
On the *piano nobile* of the Gritti e Badoer palace, this hotel is very peaceful.

Hotel Danieli
See p. 210
Riva degli Schiavoni 4191
Tel. 522 64 80
There are too many tourists on the quay, but there is a very beautiful view for breakfasts on the roof terrace. Very luxurious.

RESTAURANTS

Corte Sconta
See pp. 216–18
Calle del Pestrin 3886
Tel. 522 70 24
Take the owner's suggestions: start with the spaghetti with date mussels and finish with zabaglione and *biscotti*.

Hostaria da Franz
See p. 220
Fondamenta San Isepo 754
Tel. 522 08 61
A small trattoria that became an elegant restaurant.

Da Paolo
Campo del Arsenale 2389
Tel. 521 06 60
A small, unpretentious bistro with a sunny terrace on the pretty piazza of the Arsenale.

WINE BARS

Al Mascaron
see p. 225
Calle Lunga Santa Maria
Formosa 5225
Tel. 522 59 95
There is a counter for wine tasting and a restaurant for trying the dish of the day, such as *pasta e fagioli*.

COOKING CLASSES

Fulvia Sesani
Palazzo Morosini
Tel. 522 89 23
For learning traditional Venetian recipes and exploring the marketplace. The end of the course is marked by a grand dinner at a private palace.

SMALL MUSEUMS

Museo Storico Navale
Arsenale 2148
Tel. 520 02 76
Learn the history of the Arsenale and view a collection of boats no longer used.

**Fondazione Querini-
Stampalia**
See pp. 74, 140, 226–227
Rio Santa Formosa 4778
Tel. 522 52 35
A sixteenth-century palace restored in 1960 by Carlo Scarpa. Fine eighteenth-century furniture. A beautiful library and a pleasant garden.

BOATS

Remiera Francesco Querini
Fondamenta Nuove 6576/A
Tel. 522 20 39
Lessons are offered to club members to teach them how to row Venetian style.

MODERN ART

The Biennial of Modern Art takes place every two years (the next is in 1992) in the

Giardini Pubblici, which houses permanent pavilions for the participating nations.

GIUDECCA

HOTELS

Hotel Cipriani
Giudecca 10
Tel. 520 77 44
The perfect residence for ultra-luxurious Venetian vacations. There is a garden, a pool, and many rooms hung with Fortuny fabrics and graced with large terraces. Room number 402 probably has the best view of the two canals and of Casanova's orchard. You may sign up for the cooking lessons the hotel organizes several times a year. A hotel *motoscafo* operates between the hotel and the *piazzetta* around the clock, so clients are spared the difficulties of reaching Giudecca.

Palazzo Vendramin
Giudecca 10
Tel. 520 77 44
This Cipriani annex just opened. It offers apartments with kitchens, room service, and bars. The decor is elegant and there is a fine view of Saint Mark's Basin.

Casa Frollo
See p. 212
Giudecca 50
Tel. 522 27 23
Located at the stop of the vaporetto *Zitelle*. There are rooms with views of Saint Mark's Ba-

sin, and other, more peaceful rooms over the back garden, all decorated with antique furniture. The building is for sale: stay here before this modest pensione, with its old-fashioned charm, is too heavily renovated.

RESTAURANTS

Cipriani
See p. 213
Tel. 520 77 44
The hotel's restaurant is very pleasant for breakfast in the garden, as the sun rises over the lagoon, or lunch at poolside. The buffet offers a rich selection of specialities. The desserts are delicious.

Harry's Dolci
See p. 220
Fondamenta San Biagio 773
Tel. 522 48 44
For lunch outdoors, with the same specialties as at Harry's Bar but less expensive. *Risotto alla primavera, baccalà Mantecato* served on white polenta, and a velvety dessert, *crespelle alla crema*. Sunday lunch is very busy. Make reservations.

Altanella
See p. 221
Rio del Ponte Lungo
Giudecca 268
Tel. 522 77 80
Simple cuisine, mainly fish, to be enjoyed in a charming garden at canal level.

Do Mori
Fondamenta Sant' Eufemia 588

Tel. 522 54 52
Not far from Harry's Dolci, this good little restaurant is simpler, but has no terrace. The Zattere reflects charmingly in its window.

FABRICS

Fortuny
See pp. 200–01, 208–09
Giudecca 805
Tel. 522 40 78
The factory of the famous fabrics lies just by the Mulino Stucky, an imposing 1920s brick industrial construction, today abandoned. The Fortuny workshops are closed to the public; however, the fabrics may be seen at the Troïs boutique (*see* SAN MARCO).

SECOND-HAND SHOP

Serafin
See p. 238
Fondamenta della Croce
Tel. 522 35 48
Near the church of the Redentore, the Serafins represent generations of second-hand dealers.

BOATS

Gian Franco Vianello, aka Crea
See pp. 190–91
Fa Ponte Lungo 211/A
Tel. 523 17 98
To order a gondola or a *sandalo* . . . and win regattas. After our visit, Crea's workshop, then in Castello, moved to Giudecca. Figure on $22,000 for a gondola.

MURANO

GLASSWARE

All the famous glassmakers have their workshops on Murano. Below are some of the most interesting. They all have showrooms in SAN MARCO.

Venini
Fondamenta Vetrai 50
Tel. 73 99 55

Carlo Moretti
Fondamenta Manin
Tel. 73 92 17

Archimede Seguso
Fondamenta Serenella
Tel. 73 90 48

Barovier e Toso
Fondamenta Vetrai 28
Tel. 73 90 49

S.A.L.I.R.
See pp. 192–95
Fondamenta Manin 78
Tel. 73 90 33
The best etcher on glass. Sig. Dal Paos can make copies of the famous antique mirrors and restore antique objects.

BURANO

RESTAURANT

Da Romano
See pp. 219, 221
Via Galuppi 221
Tel. 73 00 30
A single large, lively room and a vast terrace. The Buranese come to have a drink at the counter that opens onto a very beautiful, old-fashioned

kitchen. This is the place to ask for a boat to take you to the island of San Francisco del Deserto before lunching on the terrace in the sun.

SMALL MUSEUM

Scuola Merletti
Via Galuppi
Tel. 73 00 34
Discover Venetian and *punto di Burano* lace and watch the lacemakers at work.

BOATS

Vittorio Amadi
Via San Mauro 3012
Tel. 73 00 50
They make some of Venice's most beautiful racing boats.

TORCELLO

RESTAURANTS

Locanda Cipriani
Tel. 73 01 50
Lunch on the same specialties as at Harry's Bar, in a garden overlooked by the basilica's campanile. The owner is Arrigo Cipriani's sister.

Ponte del Diavolo
Tel. 73 04 01
Traditional cuisine in rustic surroundings, by the prettiest bridge without a parapet—known as "Venetian-style."

ANTIQUES

Nicoletta Piccoli Emmer
See p. 142
Tel 73 54 69
A garden planted with sculptures across from the basilica.

LIDO

HOTELS

Hôtel des Bains
See pp. 214–15
Lungomare Marconi 17
Tel. 526 02 01
Admire the dining room's decor and the long terrace, and ruminate on Visconti and *Death in Venice.*

Quattro Fontane
See p. 214
Via Quattro Fontane
Tel. 526 02 27
An idyllic setting, a charming welcome. Rooms with themes.

Hungaria
Gran Viale 28
Tel. 526 12 12
Reasonable prices, an amusing facade.

BOATS

Circolo Canottieri Diadora
Via San Gallo 136/B
Tel. 521 34 03
Lessons are given to foreigners who want to learn how to row Venetian-style.

The drawings in this notebook are reproductions of Dionisio Moretti's nineteenth-century etchings of the Grand Canal, after Antonio Quadri's work. The original may be seen at the Biblioteca Marciana. The handmade paper that decorates the cover of this notebook comes from the Legatoria Piazzesi.

VENETIAN CALENDAR

Venice can be visited at any time of year—why not take advantage of one of its many holidays as an excuse to see it in a different season?

APRIL 25

Feast of San Marco
Offer a red rose to the one you love on this holiday, called the *Boccolo*, and have the traditional dish, *risi e bisi*, rice and peas.

MAY

The Vogalonga
Hundreds of boats await the start of this thirty-two-kilometer rowing race early in the morning of the Sunday after Ascension, on the San Marco Basin. Join in the general party atmosphere on the Cannaregio canal and try to wangle an invitation to one of the banquets that each rowing club holds.

JUNE-AUGUST

Biennial of Modern Art
Held in even years, the Biennial is an international exhibition of modern art that will lure you into the gardens of Castello.

JUNE 21

Burano Day
Regattas and the blessing of the fishing boats. Polenta and grilled fish, the food of fisherfolk, are the traditional dishes served.

JULY

Il Redentore
The Feast of the Redentore is held on the third Sunday of the month. It is possible to cross the Grand Canal on foot from Giudecca on a bridge of boats. You can watch regattas all day long, stroll beneath the Chinese lanterns that illuminate the city, and most of all, delight in the extraordinary fireworks over the San Marco Basin.

AUGUST-SEPTEMBER

Film Festival
Leave the beaches of the Lido to see the stars participating in the International Film Festival at the Hôtel des Bains and the Excelsior.

SEPTEMBER

Historic Regatta
A grand costume spectacular on the Grand Canal. A great procession of every kind of boat imaginable takes place on the first Sunday of the month. Although a reconstruction of old festivals, the Historic Regatta is also an occasion for many smaller regattas in which all the lagoon's rowing club champions participate.

NOVEMBER

Feast of the Salute
This time you will cross the Grand Canal on foot across a bridge of boats from the Gritti to the Salute. You can light candles in front of the church and buy delicious *fritelle veneziane*, fritters stuffed with raisins or pine nuts, or else enjoy mutton *castradina*.

FEBRUARY

Carnival
If you are brave enough to face the ever-increasing crowds of tourists, you can attend masques and balls throughout the city. Late at night or early in the morning, alleyways and *campi* regain some of the atmosphere of the days when Carnival lasted six months. The traditional fritters are everywhere, filled with different creams—*all crema* or *allo zabaglione*.

ACKNOWLEDGMENTS

The author expresses his most heartfelt gratitude to those who so warmly received him in Venice and allowed him to better understand and perhaps enter into their city's secrets and intimacy. He especially thanks Father Raphael Andonian, Professor Benvenuti, Claude Bernard, Bente and Pia Bevilacqua, Atalanta Bouboulis, the Contessa Ileana Chiappini di Sorio, Michele Cicogna, Sig. Crea, the Contessa Valeria Da Lisca, Sig.ra Giovanna Donati, Michele Fantini, the Contessa Maria Pia Ferri, the Contessa Franchin, Cristiano Gasparetto, François-Bernard and Edith Huyghe, Sig.ra Klinger, Peter Lauritzen, Massimiliano Longo, Tony and Marjorie Luccarda, Luciana Malgara, the Conte Girolamo Marcello, Daniele Paolin, Senatore and Sig.ra Augusto Premoli, Alvise Quarantotti-Gambini, Maria Teresa Rubin de Cervin, Connie and Natale Rusconi, Giovanni and Charlotte Sammartini, Archimede Seguso, Mario Sfriso, Giovanni Soccol, the Contessa Steiner da Schio, the Count Emile Targhetta, Sig.ra Gianfranca Totti, Sig.ra Weston, Sig.ra Luisa Zenoni-Politeo.

The photographer thanks the Contessa Marcello and her daughter Alessandra, Alvise and Auriella Dona Dalle Rose, Maria and Brandino Brandolini, and their friends Alessandro and Pascaline Barbini.

The editor thanks Nancy Novogrod, who was the first to support this project; Laure Richert, whose wide acquaintance with the city and its inhabitants was of great benefit to us; Paolo Lanapoppi, who introduced us to Venetian gastronomy; Vittoria Gosen, who was an enthusiastic and cheerful guide; Silvano Tagliapietra, who took us around the lagoon; Olivier Saillant, for the invaluable assistance he rendered Jérôme Darblay.

To all those who made invaluable contributions to the publication of this work, and especially to Gérard Julien Salvy and all those who opened their doors to the team that worked on this book: Flavio Albanese, José Alvarez, Paolo and Ketty Alvera, Didi d'Anglejan, Sig.ri Bortoluzzi, Riccardo Calimani, the Duc Descazes, Giancarlo Frulli, M. and Mme Gérard Gaussen, Andrea Grandese, Victor and Marcella Hazan, Fiora Herrera-Gandolfi, Amelie Marzato, Carlo Medioli, Pier Maria Pasinetti, Caroline Patey, Pier Luigi Pizzi and M. and Mme Regnault de la Mothe, Giovanni Roncato, Hélène Sadaune, Girolama Sammartini, Bruno Tosi, Sig.ra Vedaldi, Paolo Emanuele Zancope.

INDEX

Italic numbers refer to photographs